1974 - A WORLD IN FLUX

Joe Brydon

Gretton Books
Cambridge

First published in 2020 by Gretton Books

A CIP catalogue record for this title is available from the British Library.

ISBN   978-1-9998510-6-4 (hardback)

The publisher has no responsibility for the continued existence and/or accuracy of third party websites referred to in this book.

Printed and bound by CPI in the UK

Dedicated to everybody born since 1974
whose childhoods, working lives and retirement
are affected by the decisions taken then and since.

Older generations behaved as if the good times would last for ever.
We were mistaken and you know how wrong we were.

ACKNOWLEDGEMENTS

The work of many other people is acknowledged in the notes but I would like to pay tribute to two journalists who are no longer alive but wrote many fine articles in the 1970s and afterwards: Leo Muray, who in 1974 was political correspondent of the *Liverpool Echo* and whose perceptive articles of the time included his assessment of the year: '1974 - A vintage year for pessimists …';[1] and Keith Brace, sometime literary editor of the *Birmingham Daily Post* whose evaluation of Solzhensitsyn's criticisms of the Soviet Union in January 1974 foresaw the Nobel laureate's "crude but shrewd" expulsion from his homeland the following month.[2] Both Muray and Brace contributed to the national press in their later careers.

Cartoonists are often incisive political commentators too and a few, though not nearly enough, are represented in this book. Had it been possible, many more would have been included from across the world.

A number of people were approached by my publisher in 2019 to review individual chapters anonymously and I would like to thank those who did so. While I do not know their names, I am familiar with the astute and helpful comments that many made and I trust are reflected in the resulting text.

In addition, other people were asked earlier this year to comment on my draft in its entirety and I would like to thank the following for not only finding the time to read it but for helping it into the book it now is. Four are authors themselves of books that contributed to this study: Andy Beckett, Kenneth Morgan, Robert Skidelsky and Bill Tompson. I have benefitted from Robert Skidelsky's work on Keynes in the past, as I have from Leslie Griffiths' knowledge of twentieth century history. I sought his assistance again, as I did that of three other friends Franz Classen, Jan Haworth and David Poole, each with their particular perspectives on the time.

Several of them asked 'why 1974'? The Preface is my attempt to answer this question.

Joe Brydon
July 2020

iv

CONTENTS

PREFACE

All years are unique, some are exceptional, or in the case of 2020 'unprecedented', but 1974 was a genuinely astounding year. Many events were both a surprise and a shock, the nature and number of which had a huge and lasting impact throughout the world. 1974 stood out prominently from other years of the time in this respect. There was no single over-riding threat to norms and expectations across the world as in 2020, but it was a year of global trauma nonetheless.

In 1974 there was a general belief in supra-national organisations such as the United Nations, one that has withered and become more cynical as their authority and credibility have been blunted in the years since. Today's globalised world is founded on trade not shared values (as the escalating dispute between the west and China is making abundantly clear) and thus can be stopped at the border. Counter-intuitively, perhaps, this fosters national self-interest, concealed under the misleading banner of 'free trade', which in turn takes precedence over common interest.

The Covid-19 pandemic demonstrated that it is front-line key-workers on whom societies depend, often the most poorly paid but fundamental to everyday life. Many countries considered the protection of jobs the criterion for economic and societal health, with several putting the well-being and safety of their people, and support for their continued employment, ahead of the usual fixation on economic shibboleths - in effect a reversion to the dominant values of the 1970s, those of equalities, civil liberties and social democracy.

There are other connections. Black Lives mattered just as much in 1974, but despite the Black Power movement they and the views of minority groups were often ignored or suppressed - not just in South Africa. Colonialism was on the way out but not all countries were liberated. The superpowers now include China but the US relationship with its peers remains ambivalent and uneasy. The oil price rises of late 1973 challenged the world's way of life as climate change does today. The inter-dependence of nations, even ahead of globalisation, was apparent and people, as well as countries, better understood the advantages of this than they appear to do today. Only 1968 and 1989 might come close in that period to rivalling the epoch-shattering events of 1974.

1974 - A World in Flux

1974 CALENDAR OF EVENTS[3]

Month	Date	Country	Event
Jan	18	Egypt/Israel	Disengage along Suez Canal
	25	UK/Iran	Goods for oil exchange agreed
	27	Australia	Brisbane floods
	28	USSR/Cuba	Visit by President Brezhnev
Feb	4	UK	Eleven people killed by IRA bomb in bus on M62
	13	USSR	Solzhenitsyn deprived of citizenship and deported to West Germany
	28	UK	General election
Mar	3	France	346 people die in Paris air crash
	11	UK	Labour government ends state of emergency (from November 1973)
	12	USSR/France	Brezhnev/Pompidou summit begins
Apr	1	UK	Re-organisation of local government and NHS
	2	France	President Pompidou dies
	3	USA	President Nixon agrees to pay back unpaid income tax
	9	India/Pakistan/ Bangladesh	Foreign Ministers agree release of 195 Pakistan prisoners charged by Bangladesh with 1971 atrocities
	11	Japan	Six million workers strike
	15	Niger	Military coup
	18	USA	Subpoena issued for release of President's tape recordings in Watergate prosecution
	21	Colombia	Presidential and parliamentary elections
	24	South Africa	General election
	25	Portugal	Military coup

Calendar of Events

Month	Date	Country	Event
May	8	West Germany	Brandt resigns as Chancellor
	13	Burma	Start of strikes across the country
	15	UK	General strike called in Northern Ireland by Ulster Workers Council
	16	West Germany	Schmidt becomes Chancellor
	17	Ireland	Thirty-two people killed in Dublin car bombs
	18	Australia	General election
	18	India	Explodes nuclear device near Pakistan border
	19	France	Giscard d'Estaing elected President
	28	Italy	Eight people killed at anti-fascist demonstration in Brescia
	29	UK	Direct rule in Northern Ireland imposed after collapse of Executive
	31	Israel/Syria	Agree to disengage along Golan Heights
Jun	4	Israel	Rabin becomes Prime Minister (following Mrs Meir resignation)
	13	West Germany	Football World Cup begins
	15	UK	Red Lion Square riot
	17	UK	IRA bomb explodes in parliament
	23	Austria	Kirschläger elected President
	24	Yugoslavia/West Germany	Visit by President Tito
	26	Chile	Pinochet becomes Head of State
	27	USA/USSR	Visit by President Nixon
	29	Ethiopia	Army takes control
Jul	1	Argentina	Isabel Peron becomes President
	8	Canada	General election

1974 - A World in Flux

Month	Date	Country	Event
Jul	15	Cyprus	President Makarios overthrown
	19	Spain	General Franco hands power temporarily to Prince Juan Carlos
	20	Cyprus	Turkey invades
	23	Greece	Karamanlis returns from exile
	24	USA	Unanimous judgement by Supreme Court requires President Nixon to hand over 64 Watergate tapes
	25	Greece/Turkey/ Britain	Conference on future of Cyprus
	30	Rhodesia	General election
Aug	4	Italy	Twelve people killed by bomb on Rome-Munich express
	8	USA	President Nixon resigns
	9	USA	Ford becomes President
	11	Bangladesh	2000 people die in floods
	16	Cyprus	Ceasefire called between Turkish and Greek forces
	24	Malaysia	General election
	31	New Zealand	Prime Minister Kirk dies
Sep	6	New Zealand	Rowling becomes Prime Minister
	8	USA	President Ford pardons Nixon
	12	Ethiopia	Military coup
	19	Honduras	8000 people die in floods after hurricane
	20	Mozambique	Interim Frelimo government under Prime Minister Chissano
	30	Portugal	General Costa Gomes becomes President
Oct	5	UK	Five people killed in Guildford pub bombs

Calendar of Events

Month	Date	Country	Event
Oct	10	UK	General election
	21	Canada/France	Visit by Prime Minister Trudeau
	28	West Germany/ USSR	Visit by Chancellor Schmidt
	30	Zaire	Ali/Foreman world heavyweight boxing match
	31	South Africa	Expulsion from UN vetoed by France, UK and USA
Nov	7	UK	Two people killed in Woolwich pub bombing
	12	South Africa	Barred from UN General Assembly
	13	---	Arafat of Palestine Liberation Organisation addresses UN
	16	Ireland	President Childers dies
	17	Greece	General election
	18	USA/Japan	Visit by President Ford
	20	Kenya	Fifty-nine people die in Nairobi air crash
	21	UK	Twenty-one people killed in Birmingham pub bombs
	23	USA/USSR	Visit by President Ford
	24	Ethiopia	Sixty people executed without trial
	25	UK	IRA proscribed in Britain
	25	South Africa	Second heart transplant
	26	Japan	Prime Minister Tanaka resigns
	29	Ireland	O'Dalaigh becomes President
Dec	1	USA	Ninety-two people die in Washington, DC air crash
	4	USSR/France	Visit by President Brezhnev

1974 - A World in Flux

Month	Date	Country	Event
Dec	4	Sri Lanka	191 people die in air crash
	4	Zambia/ Rhodesia	President Kaunda hosts meeting to discuss future
	7	Cyprus	President Makarios returns
	8	Greece	Referendum on return of monarchy
	11	Rhodesia	Prime Minister Smith announces release of black political prisoners and end of guerrilla war in north
	15	France/USA	Presidents Ford and Giscard d'Estaing talks
	24	UK	Missing MP Stonehouse detained in Australia
	25	Australia	Forty-five people die in Darwin cyclone
	28	Pakistan	5000 people die in earthquake

1.   INTRODUCTION: A WORLD IN FLUX THEN

On 3rd March 1974 a Turkish Airlines DC-10 took off from Paris on the final leg of its flight to London. The plane crashed soon after when a cargo door that had not been secured properly blew out killing all 346 people on board, making it the highest death toll in any plane crash up to that point and still one of the highest ever. Human error was partly to blame but so was the design of the door, which the subsequent inquiry instructed the plane's manufacturer McDonnell Douglas to rectify. The news of this tragedy had an impact that I can still recall nearly fifty years later - both the horror of so many lives ended in a moment and the reminder that nothing should be assumed or taken for granted in life.

1974 was to reinforce this conclusion time after time and the plane's fate was both a metaphor and the message: if people were to change systems, rather than just be the victims of them, combined action would be more effective than individuals alone.

The Paris air crash may have been one of the few occasions when the otherwise ubiquitous Sheikh Yamani, front man of OPEC (the Organisation of the Petroleum Exporting Countries), was not dominating our television screens. The price of Middle East oil had almost quadrupled after the Arab-Israeli Yom Kippur war in October 1973 and was plunging the world towards recession.[4] As Barbara Castle, the politician about to join the new Labour government installed on 4th March, explained in her published diary:

> In 1974 the oil-producing countries were sucking in extra money from the rest of the world to the tune of $60 billion which their economies were unable to absorb. As their surpluses accumulated unspent, world demand was reduced."[5]

The out-going Conservative Prime Minister Ted Heath had declared a state of emergency in Britain the previous November and to reduce fuel consumption a three-day week was introduced at the end of 1973.[6] In case further conservation measures were required the Ministry of Power issued six months of petrol ration tickets to British motorists.[7] Heath's government had called a general election for the end of February 1974 on the single issue of 'Who governs Britain?' for the Conservatives assumed people would associate striking miners, exploiting the oil crisis to press their pay claim, with the Labour party. But not enough did so, for the Conservatives won more votes but fewer seats than Labour. Some people must have agreed with the Labour leader Harold Wilson that the government was over-reacting and that it was their economic mismanagement that had resulted in rising prices. It was this, Wilson argued, that the electorate should be questioning.[8] Or, as he put it in one election speech, Heath was like a naughty schoolboy pleading "please, sir, it wasn't me". Yet the answer was sufficiently unclear that Labour remained short of an overall majority.

Heath tried to hang on as Prime Minister but failed to persuade Jeremy Thorpe's Liberal Party to enter into a coalition and the Queen eventually invited Wilson to form a minority government. Wilson called an election six months later for October 1974, the first time there had been two in a year since the constitutional crisis of 1910, and this time Labour managed a bare majority over all the other parties.

There were many other elections around the world that year, some more democratic than others, as there were many other disasters, man-made and otherwise. Hurricanes in Honduras and Mexico, an earthquake in Peru and floods and a cyclone in Australia all resulted in loss of life. Hurricane Fifi left six hundred thousand people homeless in Honduras. The US President Richard Nixon resigned over Watergate in August, IRA atrocities included the Guildford and Birmingham pub bombings in October and November, Turkey invaded Cyprus following the overthrow of Archbishop Makarios by Greece, Haile Selassie was deposed as Emperor of Ethiopia in a coup that heralded seventeen years of civil war, while by contrast the rigid and authoritarian government that had ruled Portugal for almost fifty years was over-turned in a bloodless revolution led by junior military officers that eventually saw democracy introduced.[9] Isabel Peron became President of Argentina, while severe repression was underway in both Chile and Uruguay. Augusto Pinochet's name has gone down in history but Uruguay was also considered a "torture chamber", with estimates as high as 1 in 50 Uruguayans in custody and 1 in 100 ill-treated or tortured.[10] Alexander Solzhenitsyn was deprived of his Soviet Union citizenship,[11] India conducted its first nuclear test and six million Japanese workers went on strike over a wage claim. South Africa

Courtesy of *Claremont Review of Books*
Spring 2019 article on Solzhenitsyn
'The most dangerous man in the world'
© Elliott Banfield

was suspended from the United Nations in November (until 1994) for repeatedly breaching human rights and the UN Charter - though an attempt to expel them had been vetoed by the US, Britain and France, allegedly on the grounds that they did not want to see any country excluded. Elsewhere in Africa crises in Angola and Rhodesia deepened. In Asia the Soviet Union was bullying China towards policy change, with the process being repeated downstream with force being exerted by China on Vietnam and the latter in turn leaning on Kampuchea (Cambodia).[12] Diplomats would refer to this as traditional balance of power politics but it might equally be characterised as a 'pecking order'. Meanwhile the United States and the USSR were feeling their way to further détente, a word that has almost entirely disappeared from the lexicon today.

Sporting events that year included the Commonwealth Games in New Zealand and the Asian Games in Iran, but most memorable were the hosts West Germany controversially beating the Netherlands in the football World Cup final and the comeback of Muhammad Ali defeating George Foreman in Zaire, the 'Rumble in the Jungle' as it became known, to regain the world heavyweight boxing title. If the romantics were disappointed by the first result, the second compensated: a score draw for wish-fulfilment perhaps.

Denis Healey, Wilson's Chancellor of the Exchequer, described 1974 as 'a watershed in British politics'[13] but so it was in much of the rest of the world too. Many countries had to reconsider their norms and expectations in a changing world where social and cultural quakes, as well as economic ones, forced rapid readjustment. As Wilson himself put it, 'Crises are not in the habit of forming queues'.[14] Often they are interdependent and frequently intertwined; resolving one depends on first unravelling others. It was indeed a world in flux.

Coverage and Approach

1974 had opened in a subdued fashion, partly because many countries were grappling with the pre-conditions set in 1973, notably the rise in oil prices. However, this did not affect all OECD members equally (as note 4 clarifies). There was a fall in GDP per head in twenty-three out of twenty-six countries in either 1974 or 1975, but in only four of them was there a decrease in both years. As two of these countries were the UK and the USA, it has been treated by economists (at the time and since), and by the press, as of even more widespread significance than it was. It might be argued that it was the challenge to the west's place in the world hierarchy that was as threatening as the implications for its reliance on cheap oil.

While a conventional approach to the year might therefore start with a chapter on the impact of OPEC, this is deferred to Chapter 11, the penultimate chapter, before it is addressed directly. The economic and social effects are referred to in earlier chapters as they related to particular countries, but this order and approach is deliberate to avoid the implication that the effect was uniform.

Similarly, Watergate is treated both in detail in Chapter 5 and in other chapters as its disabling effects on US diplomacy determined the course of developments elsewhere (e.g., inaction over Cyprus and Vietnam, and changed relations with the USSR, Portugal and in Africa). Where the US did seem to maintain its sway to a greater extent was in South American regimes despite the humiliation of Watergate.

But there were other developments that were just as significant for national futures. These included the return of democracy to Portugal and Greece, the impact of the Portugal coup on Angola, Mozambique and Rhodesia in the restoration of autonomy and self-government, and the social market approach that characterised West Germany and Austria and provided a model elsewhere. Overarching social democracy as a fundamental, however, was the inter-dependence of countries and events. This is the thread that runs throughout the book, resulting in both direct effects in one place and equally significant knock-on effects elsewhere. There are also similarities across nations (e.g., in minority communities or the end of empire) that result in chapters, 3, 4 and 10, and continuities that remain with us today. Most notable amongst the latter, perhaps, is the contrast between UK re-negotiation of EEC membership in 1974 and the 1975 referendum with the outcome of the 2016 one and the years since.

People were increasingly aware of the international context of which they were a part and of crises in other countries across the globe. The spread of communications through greater access to television and the availability of a better informed press revolutionised people's consciousness. It is often said that Vietnam was the first televised war, but this was just a special instance of current affairs exploding into people's living rooms. The visual power of television was replicated in the growth of newspaper magazines and colour supplements, and both were augmented by the heyday of investigative reporting. People in many countries benefited from an inquiring and sceptical press that saw it as its duty to investigate the claims with which they were regaled. The contrast with today's regurgitation of a press release or soundbite could hardly be more marked.

The growth of the United Nations (UN) in the 1960s and 1970s added to this global awareness and reflected, as well as promoted, this increasing internationalism. In 1974 138 countries were represented at the UN (see Appendix), of which 51 had joined at the founding of the UN in 1945.[15] One, the Soviet Union, had not then been dismembered as it was to be in 1991, with Russia replacing it that year and the remaining eleven independent states joining then or in the following year. The founding members included fifteen countries that are covered in this book: Australia, Bolivia, Canada, Chile, Colombia, Ethiopia, France, Greece, Guatemala, Honduras, Saudi Arabia, USSR, UK, US and Uruguay. Two others, Mexico and Peru, are mentioned briefly. Ten years later there were 76 UN members, including Austria, Ireland, Italy and Portugal that had joined in the year 1955 itself and feature prominently below. The newly independent Cyprus entered in 1960, as did several African countries that had thrown off the (mainly French) colonial yoke. Many countries becoming independent from Britain, with the exception of the Indian sub-continent, Burma, Ghana and Malaysia, joined the UN in the 1960s. West Germany and East Germany were admitted in 1973, Bangladesh in 1974, Mozambique in 1975 and the re-united Vietnam in 1977. Zimbabwe joined in 1980 and features in Chapter 3 under its previous name of Rhodesia.

There are two ways of viewing this:

- either that many UN member countries are not mentioned and therefore there may be gaps (for example, China, India, much of Asia and the Middle East). Yet it would have been superfluous, as well as tedious, to have addressed them all simply for the sake of doing so. Nothing of wider significance has been omitted.

- or that countries in six of the seven continents do feature. The only continent that does not is Antarctica and the blank expanse there in 1974 is indicative of why many individual countries are not mentioned either. Things happened but not of the same scale or global importance as events in those selected.

Events are the most observable, and therefore the most obvious, markers of change, but they should also be understood as the consequence, and sometimes the culmination, of processes. This book is about some of the major events of 1974, of which there were many, but it is also about the processes that led up to them and often those that flowed from them. It would be misleading to treat events as if they could be understood separately from their historical context and future implications. Indeed, it might almost be the definition of an event as significant and worthy of public report that it cannot be meaningfully treated as if it took place in a vacuum.

Processes can be of their time, but they can transcend generations as well as countries, be lasting rather than brief, international rather than just national. That this is frequently the case for economic processes in a global world hardly needs stating, but it is often the case for social and political ones too. It is impossible to explain Northern Ireland, for example, without reference to Britain and Ireland, or Cyprus aside from Turkey and Greece, or Rhodesia apart from Portugal, Mozambique, Zambia and South Africa. All three were in turmoil for decades, and often generations, and the global superpowers then, particularly the USA but also the USSR, frequently had more than a walk-on part.

The Arab-Israeli war had brought the world within a hair's breadth of nuclear Armageddon when the USSR and US superpowers clashed. The USSR had warned Egypt not to attack Israel but wanted the US to pressurise their client state Israel to withdraw from the occupied Arab territories. However, Egypt and Syria, the other Arab country where USSR influence was strongest, agreed a war plan against Israel and on 6th October 1973 invaded. The first UN ceasefire sponsored jointly by the two superpowers failed, leading the US to threaten the USSR with nuclear war. When the next UN ceasefire held, the US-USSR crisis disappeared. Détente had not been strong enough to "prevent outbreak of the conflict … [but] it had [promoted] US-USSR co-operation in defusing [it] and preventing its escalation".[16]

This and several other examples might suggest that it was the jockeying of superpower interests that accounted for much of the conflict and confrontation across the world in 1974. This was certainly a factor, as was the triangular diplomacy which involved China alongside the US and USSR. The US aim in the Middle East was to manoeuvre the USSR out of the picture, leaving it as the one unchallenged superpower in the region.[17] Similarly the two did fight proxy wars in Africa where the USSR often enjoyed the advantage of being seen as anti-colonial by nationalist groups. In contrast, the overthrow of Allende in Chile in September 1973, as had the Arab-

Israeli war, caused the USSR to question whether the pursuit of détente with the US was meeting or hampering Soviet objectives.[18]

It would of course be naïve to underplay the significance of ideological and philosophical conflict between the US and USSR and their client states, but it would also be easy to overstate it. Capitalism's market economy felt threatened by Communism and determined not to give way to it, but there were many other examples where ecological factors such as famine or social factors such as injustice and inequality sparked uprising and revolt. External influences, including superpower relations, were important to a country's trajectory but sometimes the explanation for disruption and conflict lies predominantly in internal factors.

Furthermore, flux implies that processes interacted and that the ways in which they were handled changed the inter-dependence between them. Nor were they generally set in a mould that meant how they had been addressed previously defined how they should be tackled in the present. For example, membership of the European Economic Community (as it was then) was finely balanced nearly fifty years ago and so it is today, but how it was handled by the Labour government in 1974 is no more than a rough guide for addressing the challenges today.

And, curiously, it is not just the divisive issue of European Community membership that remains both vexed and pertinent today. Similarities continue to recur: the prospect until recently of a Presidential impeachment, with Donald Trump as today's version of Nixon, and the reality of a Turkish invasion, with the Kurds and north-east Syria providing a horrific parallel to Cyprus in 1974. Furthermore, and just as depressingly, even plane design remains subject to inappropriate corporate considerations, for in the case of Boeing in its 737-Max tragedies in Ethiopia and Indonesia in October 2018 and March 2019 respectively, the lessons had not been learned well enough or perhaps, forty-five years after the Paris air crash, had been forgotten. Institutional memory can be fragile, for ultimately it depends on people's ability not to be diverted away from the fundamental values of humanity.

2.   IN OR OUT? BRITAIN AND THE EEC

By 1973 the Bretton Woods system, in which the dollar had been pegged to gold since the end of World War II, had collapsed, with each country no longer operating a fixed exchange rate linked to the dollar. In theory, therefore, each country became more independent monetarily, but many of the weaker economies soon discovered that floating exchange rates linked to market demand were far from ideal, laying their economies open to speculation. In consequence, some decided that loss of independence was a price worth paying, preferring to link their currency to that of larger and more stable economies, usually either the dollar or mark of the US or West Germany respectively, though some of the larger economies allowed their currencies to float (Britain and Japan, for example), as did a few smaller ones that opted for a degree of monetary autonomy domestically (such as Switzerland and Canada). The implications for Britain were a decline in the dollar/sterling exchange rate of over 7% in three years from June 1972 when the pound began to float. Meanwhile, inflation initially and unemployment subsequently had both increased markedly.

A system that had been in operation for nearly thirty years had come to an end and it might be argued that this displayed increasing international confidence and national independence. The world had moved on since World War II and so should the economic and monetary arrangements that were thought vital to recovery in 1944 but were no longer so necessary in the 1970s. However, it had ended largely because of decisions taken by the US which was thereby demonstrating its global dominance, if not hegemony. It might be thought, therefore, to reflect a reduction, if not the end, of communal inter-dependence that transcended the interests of individual nations. For Britain it signalled the dilution of the much-vaunted 'special relationship', as much exercised in the breach as the observance but often the life-raft to which Britain would cling when the waves looked likely to engulf them.

In contrast a system that had been established specifically to maintain peace and avoid a repeat of senseless war in Europe was becoming stronger. As Winston Churchill had put it in May 1948 to a Congress of Europe meeting at The Hague,

> ... Mutual aid in the economic field and joint military defence must inevitably be accompanied step by step with a parallel policy of closer political unity. It is said with truth that this involves some sacrifice or merger of national sovereignty. But it is also possible and not less agreeable to regard it as the gradual assumption by all the nations concerned of that larger sovereignty which can alone protect their diverse and distinctive customs and characteristics and their national traditions.[19]

Reduced autonomy would be traded for certainty and security, and not surprisingly Churchill was not alone in identifying a unified Europe as the key to peace. For most European leaders,

> If Europe were ever to break the ruinous cycle of battles and destruction in which it had been locked for centuries, it would be by creating an institutional framework which would so bind its people together as to make armed conflict impossible.[20]

In 1950 in proposing the European Coal and Steel Community (the fore-runner of the European Economic Community) between France, Germany, Italy, Belgium, the Netherlands and Luxembourg (the latter three described collectively as the Benelux countries), Robert Schuman did so with the clear intention of making "a new war 'not only unthinkable but materially impossible'".

Almost twenty-five years later in January 1973 the original six countries in the European Economic Community (EEC) became nine with the accession of Britain, Denmark and Ireland. The strength of this grouping was further underlined in February 1975 when the EEC signed the Lomé Convention with forty-six deprived nations in Asia, the Caribbean and the Pacific, giving the latter free access for their goods to EEC markets. International inter-dependence and the recognition that long-term interests were likely to be mutual was reinforced. Twenty-two Commonwealth countries were signatories to the Lomé Convention, but all thirty-four added to the Commonwealth Conference communique that May, without consulting the British, that Britain's continued membership of the EEC was 'in the best interests of the Commonwealth'.[21] That this was in doubt was due to the re-negotiation in which the Labour government was engaged on the terms of the country's membership of the EEC and the knowledge that both the Labour party and the Labour government were split over the principle of membership at all. It was thus to Harold Wilson's credit that the re-negotiation was "confined to the terms accorded to Britain, without explicit challenge to the fundamental principles of the community".[22]

In the 1950s Europe had "courted" Britain, only to be rebuffed,[23] whereas the tables were turned in the 1960s as the President of France Charles de Gaulle vetoed Britain's application to join the EEC twice - once in 1963 when Harold Macmillan was Prime Minister and then in 1967 under Harold Wilson. Labour was preparing to re-apply once de Gaulle was replaced as President by Georges Pompidou in 1969, but it was the Heath government that capitalised on this to make the third, and this time successful, application from autumn 1970. The following September James Callaghan identified five issues that Labour would seek to re-negotiate once returned to power: the country's financial contribution; the common agricultural policy (CAP) that he said would increase food prices in Britain's shops twice as much as the Heath government claimed; the required trade barriers "against partners and kinsmen"; the risk to regional welfare, e.g., that of Wales and Scotland; and the concern that the EEC was "more favourable to those with capital to invest abroad than to those who have only their labour to sell at home".[24] Handled ineptly, these might easily have raised questions about the original Treaty of Rome and/or the principle of Britain's membership.

It would not have been feasible for the minority Labour government that took office in March 1974 to re-negotiate and a holding pattern was adopted until it gained a (slim) majority that October.[25] In a speech that December Wilson made the position clear:

> If re-negotiations are successful, it is the policy of the Labour party that, in view of the unique importance of the decision, the people should have the right to decide. If these two tests are passed ... then we shall be ready to play our full part in developing a new and wider Europe.
>
> ...
>
> [If] we get the right terms - but only if we get the right terms - I shall commend them to the British people, and recommend that we should stay in and play our full part in the development of the Community.[26]

A referendum had never been held in Britain before and when this constitutional precedent had first been suggested by Tony Benn when Labour was still in opposition, Wilson had been against it. But he came to see it as an opportunity to maintain party unity by, as Benn put it, "sub-contracting the decision to the electorate",[27] so that it was first endorsed by 8 votes to 6 in the shadow Cabinet and then by 129 votes to 96 (with more than 50 abstentions) when Wilson put it to the party.[28]

The first step before the referendum though was to achieve the re-negotiation targets Britain sought. There were now seven key areas that Wilson and Callaghan, the Foreign Secretary, pressed with the EEC:

1. the CAP and arrangements for producers outside Europe (primarily New Zealand, Australia and the Caribbean) with which Britain did the most business
2. budget contributions, which Britain wanted related to each country's gross national product (GNP) whereas all the others preferred funding through specific taxes (notably VAT)
3. monetary union, which Britain argued was "intellectually dishonest" unless it was accepted and acknowledged as only a distant objective that would require first one central bank and a single currency
4. parliamentary sovereignty (e.g., over employment), though as far back as 1961 Wilson had agreed with Churchill's view and rejected the dog-whistle absolute it has become today. The important questions were "to whom sovereignty should be ceded and for what purpose".[29]
5. capital transfers
6. developing countries
7. VAT as the way of calculating country contributions to the budget, with Britain opposed to taxing food.[30]

Callaghan first asserted these demands dogmatically but as experience in Europe increased so his tone moderated, helped in part by the death of Pompidou and his replacement by Giscard d'Estaing as French President and then in May when Helmut Schmidt became German Chancellor following the resignation of Willy Brandt. Both France and Germany became more Atlanticist in consequence,[31] with France less intransigent towards the US and Britain, and Germany more pragmatic towards the EEC.[32]

Callaghan switched away from an adversarial stance to one of "settling problems as part of the on-going business of the Community",[33] with financial support to post-revolution Portugal agreed as one such, "if, but only if, Portugal accepted a democratic solution".[34] This helped Britain to become an engaged partner in EEC discussions rather than an interested bystander, a position that was further enhanced when decisions on regional funding allocated a larger share to Britain (28%) than any other country apart from Italy (40%) and changes in global food prices made certain commodities cheaper in the EEC than outside them. If the former looked like a bribe, it was an inspired one that would be cited frequently in the forthcoming referendum.[35] When a correcting mechanism to address disparities in budget contributions was soon agreed, with Britain due a refund if their budget contribution was significantly more than its GNP-based share would imply, most of Britain's demands had been met.[36]

Wilson and Callaghan were bound to recommend approval of the negotiations even had they failed to secure the outcome they sought. But

More cynically some commentators summed it up in terms of *Realpolitik* by saying that the French wanted to keep Britain in to balance the Germans, the Germans wanted Britain to stay so as not to jeopardise the Atlantic alliance, and the rest wanted Britain in to balance Franco-German predominance.[37]

When the Cabinet considered the outcome of the negotiations, sixteen were in favour of recommending continued membership to the Commons while the seven against were allowed to disassociate publicly during the subsequent referendum as Wilson took the brave and prescient decision to suspend collective responsibility (on this one issue only) until the day after the referendum on 5th June 1975. The seven given this licence to "indulge their consciences"[38] were Michael Foot, Barbara Castle, Eric Varley, Willie Ross, Tony Benn, Peter Shore and John Silkin. Wilson had intended that they would only be allowed to abstain in the Commons vote itself but he missed the Cabinet on 25th March that permitted them to vote, though not speak, against the recommendation. It hardly mattered though for the Commons supported continued membership by 396 votes to 170. Of the latter, 145 were Labour MPs, thirty-one of them junior Ministers alongside the seven Cabinet members. Only one junior Minister spoke against the motion in defiance of a government ban on Ministers speaking in the debate. This was Eric Heffer and Wilson sacked him within the hour.[39]

There are a few similarities between the 1975 and 2016 referendums but many more differences, of which the most obvious is the outcome. In 1975 on a 67.5% turnout, 67.2% voted for continued membership and 32.8% against, with all four countries returning a clear majority, particularly so in England and Wales.[40] In other words, 45% of everybody franchised voted 'Yes'. In 2016 by contrast England and Wales voted to leave the EU and Scotland and Northern Ireland to remain. The turnout overall was higher at 72.2%, a figure exceeding that of the previous four general elections since 2001, and indicative of how strongly the country was split. 51.9% voted to leave and 48.1% to remain, barely better than the balance of probabilities standard required in civil trials, and well below the 'beyond reasonable doubt' test in criminal cases. A marginal 13:12 majority in effect, but judged sufficient in this instance to overturn more than forty years of membership. 17.41m people voted to leave and 16.14m to remain, a difference of less than 1.3m people and a knife-edge in political terms. The result would have been overturned if slightly more than half a million people had voted the other way, to remain in rather than leave the EU.

There were referenda in Quebec for independence from Canada in 1980 and 1995. On both occasions the vote was 'no', though only marginally so on the second occasion (50.6% to 49.4%). Since then Canada has changed its referenda legislation, requiring both a supermajority and the approval of both houses of parliament.[41] Although Canada has yet to clarify the clear majority that will be required in the future, there is already a precedent for this type of approach in the UK. In the 1978 votes for Scottish and Welsh devolution it was specified that a simple majority of those voting was not enough for this to be granted (technically for the enabling legislation to be enacted), for in addition at least 40% of the electorate had to vote this way. This threshold was not attained in either country. It was irrelevant in Wales where fewer than 50% of those voting sought devolution in any case, but in Scotland the majority of 51.6% for devolution was thereby nullified.

In the 2016 EU referendum 37.5% of all those franchised had voted to leave, a little over one-third of the electorate, yet no threshold had been set in advance and marginal though the result may have been it has generally been treated as decisive in the years since. In particular leading Conservative politicians, not only those who campaigned to leave, have behaved as though this was not just indicative but a mandate from the people, an instruction they were required to follow regardless of the economic and social damage that might result. In 1975 Harold Wilson noted that the referendum then could not be binding on MPs though he believed that "not many Members would pit their judgement against a decision by the country".[42] Presumably a subtle and pragmatic politician such as Wilson, however, would accept that for most MPs this would depend on how clear-cut the decision was both in their local area and overall. Since 2016 many MPs have not only paid attention to the strength of feeling in their local constituency but have behaved as though half the country did not exist. A politician to his core such as Wilson, interested in people rather than profits, would have realised that he would have little future if he disenfranchised half the people in this way. He did not wear blinkers and was not the ostrich that some of those in parliament appear to be today. Some of them have already found out the hard way that choosing blinkers or the ostrich option may bring short-term benefits but ultimately is career-limiting.

A second key difference is that people knew what they were voting for in 1975 with the terms having been re-negotiated in advance. In 2016, after David Cameron's shuttle round Europe produced no meaningful change, they did not. People had little choice in 2016 but to vote with their heart rather than their head, with some no doubt indicating their emotional attachment to Europe and the advantages that European citizenship brought, whereas others may have felt ignored or left behind by the British or European establishments. That this was an emotional decision for many is demonstrated by the campaign for remain, 'Project Fear' as it was dubbed, stirring up anxieties about leaving rather than promoting the benefits of remaining. Others may have voted for specific reasons around immigration, control of borders or the supposed 'sovereignty' that Britain could regain.

That this is supposed rather than actual 'sovereignty' is demonstrated by the EU only reaching decisions and agreeing change on the basis of unanimity in what are considered 'sensitive' areas by the member states.[43] Britain has always had the option to vote against, and hence veto, anything with which it disagreed. This was always sufficient on its own to prevent implementation. Sovereignty can only be lost where disagreement with a particularly critical and far-reaching change is insufficient to prevent it coming into effect. The opt-out from the social chapters of the Maastricht Treaty that Britain secured in 1992 demonstrates that there was also an intermediate option that the EU were prepared to concede.

Whatever the factors that informed the decisions of individual voters in 2016, however, perhaps the most significant feature is that, because the outcome was not clear-cut and beyond dispute, a wide variety of interpretations have been chosen by MPs and commentators to suit their own ends. Some people may have voted against European immigration, and the reduced job opportunities that resulted for the indigenous population in some areas, but in most instances Britain has benefited hugely from immigration and, in the service and agricultural sectors in particular, the country's dependence on it will soon become apparent once we leave. Those opposed to immigration prefer this explanation for the outcome, while others refer to communities that may have felt 'left behind' if they did not receive EU funding or derived no benefit from the financial hub that is London. The explanation here is that these people gave the establishment "a good kicking". Staggeringly, some may even have hankered after Empire and the days when Britain supposedly stood alone. For these people even "Dunkirk was a victory, if only because it got us out of Europe".[44]

A third key difference was the position adopted by the Prime Ministers in the referendum campaign. Wilson had made his intentions clear in advance but during the campaign itself he "held himself aloof. He gave statesmanlike speeches to selected audiences, advocating a 'Yes' vote. But he let others do the proselytizing".[45] Cameron by contrast was in the fray, one of the leaders of the 'Yes' campaign alongside his Chancellor Osborne. The consequence was that when the result went against him his credibility was shot and he resigned on the morning afterwards. Osborne soon followed.

Both Wilson and Cameron had been attracted by a referendum that would help them to maintain party unity - for Wilson by papering over the differences in the Cabinet and the Labour Party, for Cameron by keeping his 'awkward squad' of backbenchers who wanted to leave the EU quiet during the 2015 general election. Cameron never expected to be in a position to have to deliver on his promise but no doubt reassured himself that the British people would vote for continued peace and prosperity. That they did not has once again highlighted the breaches in the Conservative party over Europe, but this time has taken the country down too. It threatens the union of the United Kingdom and it limits the prospects of all those who still have a working life ahead of them.

One political commentator wrote in March 1975 that Wilson had three objectives: "to keep his party in power and in one piece and Britain in Europe".[46] He succeeded in all of them, whereas Cameron and his immediate successors may not manage even one.

Interestingly, and perhaps presciently in view of the debates about EU membership that took place in the UK ahead of the 2016 referendum, Georges Pompidou, the French President at the time of Britain's entry, had welcomed the UK joining as he thought it would bolster Europe, whereas it is claimed that a contrary view in France was that Britain "would delay political integration and would want to transform the great European project into a free trade zone".[47] After fifty years of benefiting from increasing integration (of people as well as politics), and this being more significant than geography and loose alliances based mainly on trade, the country is about to return to the latter. Britain will remain a European nation of course, but whether it will become increasingly marginalised, a small country on the sidelines as well as on the edge of Europe, remains to be seen.

3. **MINORITY COMMUNITIES AND INTERVENING, OR FAILING TO: CYPRUS, RHODESIA AND NORTHERN IRELAND**

To paraphrase John Donne, not even "an island is an island". There are several senses in which this was the case for Cyprus in July 1974 when Turkey mounted an invasion, or to some minds a peace-keeping operation, to protect the minority Turkish Cypriot community from further attacks by the majority Greek Cypriots.[48] As in Northern Ireland a minority community was suffering at the hands of its majority neighbours and outside protection or intervention (the British on behalf of the Catholic community in 1969 in Northern Ireland) would be fundamental to the subsequent course of events.

The bloodless revolution in Portugal would reverberate not only in its colonies of Angola and Mozambique as they sought independence but would prove the catalyst for change in Rhodesia too. The removal of Mozambique as a buffer "convinced [South Africa] that Rhodesia had become dispensable within the changed balance of power in southern Africa ..." as that country sought "better relations with independent Black Africa". [49] White Rhodesia might wish to preserve its settler way of life in isolation from the currents of self-determination that swirled around it, but by 1974 it was becoming clear that black majority rule was likely if not inevitable.

In contrast to the outside interventions in Cyprus and Northern Ireland, therefore, it was the withdrawal of external support that, alongside the increasing black guerrilla action, changed Rhodesia's future. So, in between the two extremes represented by the collapse of the Bretton Woods agreement and the signing of the Lomé Convention, each striking in opposite ways at the cardinal principles that underpinned the world order, it was events in one of the less populated countries of Europe that would have a powerful effect in southern Africa.

Cyprus

The fate of Cyprus was significant not only to the two superpowers in 1974, the USA and the Soviet Union, but to many other countries throughout the world that had minority problems of their own.

19

Alongside the 1960 constitution under which the independent Republic of Cyprus had been established, there were three Treaties of which the Treaty of Guarantee was the most critical. This guaranteed that Britain, Greece and Turkey would protect the 'sovereignty, territorial integrity and independence' of Cyprus and could intervene in the event of this being threatened, internally or externally. While such intervention was expected to be joint, any of the three countries could intervene unilaterally to re-establish the 1960 constitutional position.[50]

Clashes between the two communities on the island had taken place since 1963 when the Greek Cypriot leader Archbishop Makarios proposed amendments to the 1960 constitution.

The constitution required the Greek and Turkish Cypriots to share power as equal partners. This had never happened, but Makarios' 13-point plan in November 1963 had the explicit aim of bringing about union between Cyprus and Greece and depriving Turkish Cypriots of their basic rights in the process. Not surprisingly, the Turkish Cypriots did not accept this, giving the Greek Cypriots the excuse they were seeking to attack the Turkish community. In four days 30,000 Turkish Cypriots had to evacuate 103 villages and hundreds lost their lives. Turkey failed to get Britain and Greece, the other two guarantor powers under the 1960 Treaty, to act and, though Turkey's warning flights brought the immediate bloodshed to an end, the upshot was Greek Cypriot rule from 1963 to 1974, with Turkish Cypriots ousted from the administration.[51]

According to one authority on the Cyprus conflict, "It has been said that [the Greek Cypriots] cannot remember what happened between 1963 and 1974, and the Cypriot Turks cannot forget".[52]

On 15th July 1974 Archbishop Makarios was overthrown by a coup orchestrated by the Greek junta for he had spoken of "achieving not what was desirable, but what is feasible" which was interpreted in Greece as deferring union for some time. Makarios fled the island and the Greek Cypriots started massacres again. Another 16,000 Turkish Cypriots had to abandon another 38 villages. Five days later Turkey intervened militarily under the Treaty of Guarantee.[53] The UN required the three guarantor nations to negotiate to restore peace but the first Geneva conference at the end of July failed to curtail attacks on Turkish Cypriots and a second Geneva conference in August was equally ineffective. Consequently, Turkey launched phase two of its intervention to protect Turkish Cypriots in the south. This lasted three days and eventually the Turkish Federated State of Cyprus was proclaimed in the north in February 1975 (the Turkish Republic of North Cyprus since 1983). This left the possibility of federation with the south in due course but it has never happened.[54] Perhaps as many as 200,000 Greek Cypriots had been displaced from the north and 50,000 Turkish Cypriots from the south, with 4000 and 1000 deaths on each side respectively.[55] The two zones remain in separate operation today.

Despite being one of the three guarantor nations, Britain had kept "as low a profile as possible",[56] slip-streaming in the wake of US diplomacy, a stance for which it was roundly condemned in a Select Committee report in August 1976. Although a British diplomat has characterised this report as "shallow and prejudiced",[57] it has been described elsewhere as "one of the deadliest works of criticism".[58] Intervention might have risked the future of Britain's bases on the island, a strategic as well as tactical consideration, but non-intervention risked its strategic and diplomatic credibility, as well as its moral authority on the world stage.

The USA and the US Secretary of State Henry Kissinger had dilemmas of their own which events elsewhere amplified.

Cyprus was of strategic importance to the USA because on the one hand they feared it might become a Mediterranean Cuba if Turkey called in the Soviet Union to support their 1974 invasion[59] and on the other for the defence of Israel, particularly following the Yom Kippur war.[60] On both counts the US historically favoured the Greek military junta run by the Colonels since 1967: because they were anti-communist and because the US had signed a five-year agreement with them in January 1973 to secure access to port facilities at a time when other options in the Mediterranean were closed to them. This annoyed Arab countries, of course, but the Greek government did not go so far as to recognise Israel.

Secondly, US foreign policy was confused over Greece for, though the long-term aim of the State Department, and possibly the Central Intelligence Agency (CIA) as well, was the restoration of democracy, in the short-term Greece was a useful buffer against

Soviet Union expansion. By contrast the Soviet Union "favoured a non-aligned, independent Cyprus, free of foreign influence".[61]

Thirdly, the US was inhibited from a coherent policy position at the time of Turkey's invasion because of the fall-out from the Watergate scandal. This is the justification Kissinger used to explain US inaction so that Turkey was "enabled to invade with impunity".[62] The Soviet Union did not criticise Turkey because the invasion itself would irritate Turkey's NATO allies and this was a dispute they did not want to see diluted. Subsequently, the second Geneva conference to seek a peaceful settlement between Greek and Turkish Cypriots started the same day Nixon resigned, 8th August 1974. It soon collapsed.[63]

Rhodesia

If Cyprus was complex, Rhodesia was more so, though there were obvious similarities such as an obdurate leader holding to a morally indefensible position and not prepared to listen to other views.

Faced with the prospect of black majority rule in 1965, as Britain's other colonies in Africa had achieved with independence, white Rhodesia refused to countenance this and espoused UDI (Unilateral Declaration of Independence) instead. The wily Prime Minister Ian Smith and his Rhodesia Front party would not accept indigenous government for it threatened the comfortable lifestyle and advantages enjoyed by the white community. They held out the threat of black anarchy, but in reality were shrinking from the levelling up this would lead to for the black community and the altered status that the whites would have to accept in consequence. Harold Wilson held talks twice with Smith in subsequent years (on HMS Tiger in 1966 and on HMS Fearless in 1968) and

> By the end of the 1960s an extensive [British and UN] boycott was allegedly in force. Yet without the co-operation of Portugal and South Africa no sanctions policy could be properly effective ...[64]

The Conservative Prime Minister Ted Heath and his Foreign Secretary Lord Home (a previous Conservative Prime Minister himself as Alec Douglas-Home) re-opened negotiations in 1971, but if the British thought they had made progress they soon became aware that Smith put a different gloss on the outcome. A peace commission was established in 1972 but this too led nowhere and in effect the British had washed their hands of the situation by the time Wilson returned to power in 1974.

By contrast South Africa had maintained positive relations with its neighbour until the April 1974 coup in Portugal irrevocably altered the situation. "Rhodesia had become an obstacle to South Africa's plans for détente in southern Africa."[65]

Mr Vorster, the Prime Minister of South Africa, understood the implications … far-reaching change was imminent in southern Africa, the Republic could no longer depend upon White buffer status to defend its borders, Pretoria would have to establish good relationships with the Black governments constituting the Front Line States. The immediate problem was Rhodesia.[66]

Meanwhile, in an attempt to insulate black Rhodesians from the terrorists, the Rhodesian government had started a programme of 'protected villages' in 1973, extending it in mid-1974.[67] However, this was not about protecting existing villages close to the Zambian and Mozambique borders in the north-east, making it harder for terrorists to infiltrate and bully or torture the inhabitants. Rather it was about moving people from their existing homes in these areas to barbed wire encampments where they were given a small patch of land on which they often had to build a shelter with whatever materials they could collect, and might have to dig a new well and toilet. They were allowed out during the day to tend their crops or animals, often now some miles away, but a curfew operated from 6pm to 6am. This approach was "borrowed from the British in Malaya (where it worked) and from Algeria, Vietnam, and Mozambique (where, generally, it did not)",[68] and was symptomatic of Rhodesian thinking in at least two senses: firstly, officers who had fought with the British in Malaya twenty years earlier adopted wholesale a strategy that had worked then even though it had failed elsewhere in the interim and might not be appropriate in the Rhodesian circumstances in any case; and, secondly, what mattered was the protection of whites and their way of life, with the black population treated harshly and inhumanely regardless. This attests to the strength of Godwin and Hancock's assertion that "most [white] Rhodesians reacted to the new circumstances by affirming the dominant values of the past".[69]

Not surprisingly, the 'protected villages' strategy was counter-productive and self-defeating, not least because "physical isolation of civilian Blacks [sic]"[70] was the basis for assessing success, rather than improvements to their standard of living, which it singularly failed. Had quality of life been targeted instead it might well have separated the black population from the terrorists and kept them apart more effectively. Such a *volte face* was never likely, however, for it would have required Smith's government to adopt an enlightened approach to its black majority, treating them more equitably (perhaps even equivalently to the white minority), that would have struck at its assumption of superiority and cut across its fundamental beliefs and basic values.

Courtesy of Pitts Theology Library, Candler School of Theology, Emory University, Joseph Morgan Johnson Political Cartoons
Umbowo October 1974[71]
© Joseph Morgan Johnson

Between 1967 and the end of 1974 South Africa had increased the number of South African police (SAP) working in Rhodesia to help the country protect its borders from 300 to 2000. They had a practical value in freeing up Rhodesian manpower for other security functions but their symbolic value to white Rhodesia was at least as great. After the Portugal coup the whole South African strategy changed. With Angola and Mozambique heading towards black rule, and with "white rule [in Rhodesia] ultimately doomed" in President Vorster's view, Smith and white Rhodesia had become a liability. The country was no longer the front-line of defence against any external threat to South Africa and its unstable, white government was less appealing than a stable, and preferably moderate, black one.[72] Vorster and President Kaunda of Zambia embarked on a programme of détente that would bring about a transition to black majority rule in Rhodesia. According to Meredith, Zambia persuaded Vorster to withdraw the SAP from Rhodesia on the pretext of a ceasefire agreement between Rhodesia and the guerrillas provided the front-line black states prevented the guerrillas using Rhodesia as a base through which to attack South Africa.[73] For Godwin and Hancock, however, Vorster withdrew the SAP in February 1975 when Smith reneged on the "understanding that had underwritten détente: namely ... a common roll based on a qualified franchise and the notion of power-sharing".[74] In his autobiography Rhodesia's intelligence chief Ken Flower similarly refers to this breakdown of Smith/Vorster relations as a result of "Smith's reversal of stated policies".[75] Despite Rhodesian pleas, Vorster withdrew the SAP completely. The impact on white morale in Rhodesia was huge as can be seen from Smith accusing the South African government of "doubletalk" that September for, he claimed, they had previously promised to retain the SAP in Rhodesia until terrorism ceased.[76] Clearly any special relationship between Smith's Rhodesia and South Africa was, if not yet completely over, severely and perhaps irreparably damaged.

As Barbara Castle recorded in her diary for 5th December 1974:

At Cabinet Jim [Callaghan] reported that Vorster was beginning to put pressure on Ian Smith to reach a settlement with the Africans in Rhodesia. Clearly events in Portugal had made South Africa realize she must come to terms with black Africa. There was now the possibility of a constitutional conference, though the joker in the pack was still Smith, as we well knew.[77]

Earlier in July 1974 Smith's Rhodesia Front had secured a clean sweep in the (white) polls and in the year as a whole the economy grew by 10% despite external factors such as "sanctions … the rise in oil prices [and] the advancing world recession," as well as internal uncertainty and anxiety.[78] Consequently, most whites "accepted Smith's view that a settlement was still desirable but not essential".[79] However, not even "the Lisbon coup seemed to change the [Rhodesian] government's perception of what a settlement might mean, or to inject any note of urgency into its negotiations."[80] This would soon change as the war started up again from January 1975 and the economic growth of 1974 proved to be the last.

Northern Ireland

'The troubles', as this phase of the longstanding and continuing dispute in Northern Ireland is generally known, were less bloody than the conflicts in Cyprus and Rhodesia, but in 1974 it was not clear that this would be the case. The first regiment of British troops had been deployed on the streets of Northern Ireland in 1969 at the request of the Stormont (i.e., Northern Ireland) government. Violence in Northern Ireland peaked in 1972, as Table 1 shows, but remained distinctly 'bloody' in 1974. Although the terror had been exported directly to England before, firstly in October 1971 when a bomb had been planted at the Post Office Tower and then in March 1973 when car bombs outside the Old Bailey resulted in one person dead and nearly 250 people injured,[81] it was in 1974 that it became widespread for the first time. The M62 bomb in February killed eleven, while the Guildford, Woolwich and Birmingham pub bombings later in 1974 resulted in twenty-seven dead and over 250 injured. While each of these atrocities was the work of the Provisional IRA, the Protestant Ulster Volunteer Force unleashed three car bombs in Dublin in May, killing twenty-two people and injuring over 100.[82] The term "injured" downplays what was often a life-changing trauma, with the loss of limbs and permanent disfigurement not uncommon.

The number of dead and wounded is in any case only one measure of the 'bloodiness' of a conflict; the suspension of normal life for the law-abiding majority might be another, with checkpoints a disruption but bombs and the constant fear and threat of terror rather more; while a third might be a growing divide at the heart of the community that, whatever the intentions of the authorities, was widening not narrowing. As in Cyprus and Rhodesia, homes became unsafe and thousands were forced to move, or felt they had to, because they lived in 'the wrong place'. In areas of Londonderry and Belfast physical barriers were erected to keep Catholic and Protestant communities apart for their own protection. Known as 'the peace line', this was similar to the Turkish enclave carved out in northern Cyprus or protected villages in Rhodesia. Each was an approach that might make the situation more manageable in the short-term but did nothing to provide a solution for the long-term.

Year	Deaths	Shootings	Bombs planted
1969	13	NA	8
1970	25	213	170
1971	174	1756	1515
1972	467	10,628	1853
1973	250	5018	1520
1974	216	3206	1113
1975	247	1805	635

Table 1: Deaths, shootings and bombs planted in Northern Ireland 1969-1975[83]

This is not to say that long-term solutions were not sought. As early as November 1968 a five-point reform package was announced to respond to the most pressing grievances of Catholics over their civil rights. It included the allocation of housing according to need by local authorities, the appointment of an Ombudsman to investigate people's complaints, a development commission to replace the Londonderry corporation, the repeal of the Special Powers Act (still in operation from the 1920s) as soon as it was "safe to do so", and the reform of local government.[84] This package of reforms had been pressed on the O'Neill, Craig and Faulkner triumvirate at the head of the Northern Ireland government by Harold Wilson, responding on behalf of a British government appalled at the excessive force used by the police against a civil rights march in Londonderry the previous month, a reaction that had been equally sharp in Dublin.[85] For Bew and Gillespie it was this confrontation between the Northern Ireland Civil Rights Association (NICRA) and the police that "opened up the modern Ulster crisis".[86] On 5th October 1968 about 500 NICRA protestors,

> were joined by Gerry Fitt, Eddie McAteer and some British Labour MPs. The RUC [Royal Ulster Constabulary] had gathered in large numbers to make sure [the] march would not cross Craigavon Bridge and enter [Derry]. The leaders of the march were violently attacked by the RUC and many were seriously injured … The event was filmed by an RTE film crew and later that evening … was on television news across Europe and the world.[87]

From the original call by the Northern Ireland government in August 1969 for the British army to patrol the streets and protect the Catholic community, there were 19 army units by 1972, up from 7 units and 7000 men (even fewer originally) as disorder escalated. Internment, in other words imprisonment without trial, had been introduced in 1971, making tension and violence between the communities worse, and with the Stormont parliament suspended from March 1972 Northern Ireland came under direct rule from Westminster. Internment and direct rule played into the hands of the Provisional IRA who saw these as steps to a united Ireland, whereas the measures taken to ameliorate Catholic grievances were perceived by many in the Protestant community as challenging their historic ascendancy. Hard men on both sides, and the plethora of violent groups, had the upper hand.

The contrast with the previous IRA campaign called off in 1962 could not be more marked. Then the government of Northern Ireland had remained "firm but calm", preventing both reprisals in the north and counter-attacks across the border.[88]

By 1974 the British army had overall responsibility for security, even though the aim had been to give the police primacy. The Northern Ireland Police Act implemented from March 1970 had intended that the police be unarmed but by March 1971 they had been handed back their guns and drove around in armoured cars as violence grew and law and order deteriorated.[89]

The Police Act was only one part of a reform package designed to defuse tensions. In May 1973 the first elections were held for the new district councils, no longer responsible for the development or allocation of housing that had proved so divisive, and the following month, again by proportional representation, for a power-sharing Assembly. Forty-nine Unionists were elected to the 78 seats in the Assembly, not enough to form the Executive according to the rules and in any case in three groupings that frequently disagreed (22 Official Unionists committed to Faulkner and 27 others split between Craig's Vanguard movement and Paisley's DUP). What all the Unionists did agree on though was opposition to power-sharing, which they saw as capitulating to the Republican cause, while the 22 SDLP members were only prepared to participate in the Executive if internment was ended. Yet, despite these apparently irreconcilable positions, an eleven member Executive was formed of six Unionists, four SDLP and one Alliance member, with Faulkner as the Chief Executive designate and Fitt as his deputy.[90]

The Executive collapsed before it got going, brought down by three events. Firstly, after much pressure from the SDLP for a Council of Ireland the British and Irish governments had reached the Sunningdale agreement in December 1973, but the following month the Ulster Unionist Council rejected it. Faulkner resigned as putative Chief Executive. Secondly, the general election at the end of February 1974 was focussed on the economy in the rest of the UK but on the Sunningdale agreement in Northern Ireland. The United Ulster Unionist Council, which had been formed in January in order to bring down the Executive, took 51% of the vote and, under the first past the post system, eleven of the twelve seats in Northern Ireland. Thirdly, in March the Ulster Workers Council threatened "widespread civil disobedience unless fresh Assembly elections [were] held", a call they repeated on 10th May. Four days later they called a strike in protest at Assembly support for the Sunningdale agreement. Over the next fortnight Northern Ireland was brought to its knees, largely because of the workers' control over power stations and thus the electricity supply. The strike was called off on 29th May when the prospect of a Council of Ireland had been removed and the following day the Assembly was prorogued.[91]

As Buckland notes, the Provisional IRA had moved from defence of the Catholic community to attack in February 1971 and it was mainly their violence that ended the Protestant regime at Stormont in 1972, while the strike of Protestant workers had brought down the Assembly and its Executive in 1974: "Extra-constitutional protest had destroyed two constitutions and was always likely to destroy others in the future."[92]

Nearly twenty-five years later the Belfast or 'Good Friday' agreement was signed in 1998 but the British army remained on active service in Northern Ireland until July 2007, two years after the date had been confirmed in response to the Provisional IRA announcing that their campaign was over. There were three aspects to the agreement: the establishment of a directly-elected Assembly in Northern Ireland; cross-border co-operation between Northern Ireland and the Republic; and continued consultation between the British and Irish governments. When the agreement was put to a vote in May 1998 across all of Ireland, it was endorsed by 94% of voters in the Republic and by 71% in Northern Ireland. Within the latter figure, however, 96% of Catholics supported the agreement whereas only 52% of Protestants did.[93] None of the elements in the agreement were new but finally a majority in both communities supported them.

4.   THE CENTRE CANNOT HOLD: IMPERIAL DECLINE IN ETHIOPIA AND EMPIRE DECLINE IN ANGOLA, MOZAMBIQUE AND VIETNAM

It may not be obvious why Vietnam is included in the same chapter as three African countries, not least because by the end of 1974 US involvement on the ground in Vietnam had virtually ceased, but there are both parallels and a clear link that make this not only understandable but unavoidable.

First, the parallels: Angola and Mozambique were two of Portugal's colonies in Africa (the other main one was Guinea-Bissau) but, unlike Britain and France, Portugal thought of these as provinces rather than separate countries in their empire (imperial possessions).[94] This had consequences during the Portuguese occupation and then when the countries became independent in 1975. During the occupation many of the managerial and technical posts went to Portuguese nationals and there was an absence of African education. The upshot was that when the Portuguese withdrew ahead of independence, virtually overnight, both countries were left without the skilled human resources their economies required. Many enterprises closed almost immediately as a result. Similarly, South Vietnam had become reliant on US (military) skills and resources and when US policy switched towards *Vietnamisation* of the war, leaving South Vietnam to face the North almost alone, it did not take long for South Vietnam to collapse in 1975. South Vietnam was never an American colony, of course, but it was a buffer against Soviet and communist expansion in Asia just as Angola and Mozambique were buffers against black Africa and guerrillas for South Africa and its occupation of South West Africa (later Namibia). South Africa and the US (CIA) often acted in concert in funding guerrilla groups to fight each other (e.g., the FNLA and UNITA against the MPLA in Angola), thereby disabling the spread of Marxism-Leninism and distracting them from overthrowing the apartheid regime in South Africa.

Ethiopia, on the horn of Africa, was distant geographically from the other three countries and was one of only two on the continent never to be colonised by European powers (the other was Liberia) - though it was of course occupied briefly by Italy when it was still known as Abyssinia. Despite the Emperor Haile Selassie's appeal to the League of Nations to deter the Italian dictator Mussolini, the international community did nothing and Britain and France (through the Hoare-Laval pact) were complicit in Italy's aggression. Nevertheless, until its collapse in the 1970s Ethiopia was an empire where the Emperor was the ultimate authority and arbiter, whose word was law and where the population did his bidding. This is the same role as the USA has assumed, particularly since the Second World War, to protect its interests and while it would justify such a stance as deterring Soviet or Chinese communist takeover, not for nothing does Noam Chomsky call his analysis of American imperialism 'Deterring Democracy'. Self-determination was only acceptable to the US administration to the extent that it entailed endorsement and acceptance of the US approach. Consequently, Chomsky refers disparagingly to an article in *Foreign Affairs* that attempted to explain the foundering of US-Soviet détente by reference to Vietnam, Angola and Ethiopia.[95] Furthermore, like Portugal in Angola and Mozambique, education in Ethiopia was limited to the requirements of the system. There were few graduates and for most of the rural population it ended at elementary school (assuming they accessed it at all).

Secondly, the link: Following US humiliation in Vietnam, the American Senate passed what is known as the Clark Amendment (Dick Clark was the Iowa senator who sponsored it) specifically to prohibit US funding of anti-Communist groups and so prevent the USA becoming embroiled in such Cold War conflict again. This was "the high point of a congressional revolt against the anti-Communist ethos of the Cold War and executive authority in foreign policy".[96] It was the Clark Amendment that was supposed to have brought US involvement in Angola to an end - though the CIA continued to be involved covertly,[97] with the CIA programme manager for Angola John Stockwell confirming that the Agency lied about this to Congress and to the committee supervising the Angola programme.[98]

Ethiopia

The Ethiopian monarchy stretched back nearly two thousand years with Haile Selassie Emperor since 1930 and regent prior to that from 1916. When he was deposed in September 1974 he had been in power for 58 of his 82 years, apart from a brief period of exile after the country was invaded by Italy in 1936,[99] and he and Ethiopia were often thought of in the same breath, almost as synonymous. Consequently, when things went badly wrong he was the person to blame and indeed, as an absolute monarch, the accountability was often his. René Lefort, the French journalist who has observed developments in Ethiopia since the 1970s and was deported by the Ethiopian authorities in November 2017,[100] included some telling aphorisms in his book on the revolution.[101] For example, the 1973 "famine tore apart the view of modernity with which the Emperor had cloaked his reign" for rising food prices affected the new urban population of Ethiopia as well as those in rural areas.[102] Not all parts of the country were equally affected, with drought in seven of Ethiopia's fourteen provinces,[103] but rather than re-direct surpluses in the south to the northern areas that suffered first, the regime tried to downplay the significance of the famine. Aid was eventually requested from the west but such requests were whispered so as not to panic the country as a whole. As Keller put it, the "government wanted and needed aid, but it wanted it on the quiet".[104] A UNICEF survey was suppressed by the regime in mid-1973 and it was only when Jonathan Dimbleby's film for Thames TV's *This Week* was shown in London in October 1973 that European audiences became aware of the full horror and extent of starvation in the country.[105] Almost as alarming was the contrast it presented of a backward and undeveloped country so at odds with the modernising image that Haile Selassie had sought to project abroad. The Emperor visited the area himself in November 1973, a year after the rains had failed, yet despite being "genuinely appalled" by what he saw it would be another year (and therefore after he had been deposed) before a state of emergency was declared.[106] Up to two hundred thousand people starved to death.

The grain supply crisis was exacerbated by hoarding and a population that for the first time exceeded Ethiopia's ability to feed it. Food prices rose and were compounded by the international increase in oil prices and by inflation. Several army garrisons were in dispute over both their living conditions and pay, while various elements of the Addis Ababa population (from students to teachers to transport workers) were in revolt. To quote another of Lefort's aphorisms, the consequent "demand overload" was well beyond the capacity of a decrepit regime to handle.[107] In several instances Haile Selassie, rather than his government, caved into the demands, thereby reacting in a way which encouraged and legitimised further protest while at the same time exposing the political fig-leaf that was the Prime Minister and the Cabinet. And, in addition, ethnic and religious tensions came to the surface, further fuelling the long-standing demands for self-determination of peoples and regions that had been sublimated while the regime appeared in command. Eritrea was the most obvious of these, for though it had become the fourteenth province of Ethiopia in 1962, its demands for self-determination had never disappeared. Even with Haile Selassie's removal, "the Ethiopian revolution was ... already chained to a millstone, the 'Eritrean question'. The oldest armed national liberation struggle in Africa".[108]

Keller sets out the long-standing education and health inequalities that favoured the Addis Ababa and Amhara regions over the rural and non-Amharic, or non-ruling, populations.[109] For example, there were only sixty-one secondary schools in the country in 1972, one in four of which were in the province that surrounded and included the capital city, as were twenty-five of the eighty-five hospitals, thirteen of them in Addis Ababa itself. By contrast 80% of the population did not have access to modern medical services and 9% of the country's hospitals served 25% of its population across six southern provinces. To absolute deprivation in much of the country, therefore, was added the injustice of inequalities and heightened deprivation among some groups and in some areas. Keeping these from boiling over depended on continued subjugation that restricted people's horizons and made them accept their lot in case the alternative was worse. This might be achieved by a violent and repressive regime (as happened under Mengistu in Ethiopia later and elsewhere in Africa) but could also result from institutionalised and coercive systems that had developed over time, such as the feudal systems of land tenure and the subsistence existence of most people in the case of Haile Selassie's Ethiopia, that kept the peasants focussed on their survival each day rather than imagining a different tomorrow.

There were other proximate causes of the 1974 revolution that, fourteen years after the first attempt, threw out the Ethiopian

Emperor and his regime. Martin Meredith summarises his long rule and, to Western eyes, his remarkably swift demise in a few pages.[110] The oil shortage and inflated prices for imports led the regime to embrace austerity, notably through educational reform that choked off the few urban career options available to the limited number of graduates the system produced and encouraging them to return to rural areas instead. In many instances they would have to pay fees for this as well. Teachers had been seeking a pay increase since 1968 but five years on it had still not been resolved. They threatened to strike while students actually did so. Petrol was rationed and pump prices increased while taxi drivers were forbidden to raise the rates they charged.[111] Army grievances escalated and, rather than suppressing dissent, they often made common cause with other disgruntled groups. In February 1974 army salaries were increased and two days later the petrol price rise, education proposals and price controls generally were all suspended.[112]

The regime appeared weak and indecisive, the army grievances became increasingly political and the Cabinet resigned at the end of February 1974. Haile Selassie then promised a new constitution within six months, with the Prime Minister to be responsible for the first time to parliament rather than the Emperor, and student demands for an end to press censorship were agreed. Next the Confederation of Ethiopian Labour Unions (CELU) made their own demands, notably for a minimum wage, calling a general strike, including by government employees who were supposed to be banned from striking. The strike was called off on 11th March, four days after it had started, when the regime capitulated.[113]

And so the "creeping revolution" crept on (i.e., advanced slowly), with one other significant difference from the abortive coup of 1960. Then the army had been factionalised and divided, both within its own ranks and from other groups, whereas in 1974 a military co-ordinating committee (Derg) was established in June, chaired eventually by Major Mengistu Haile Mariam and under a slogan around which all groups could rally of 'Ethiopia First'. When Haile Selassie agreed to the Derg's five demands in July, it supplanted the "nominal civilian cabinet" as the power in the land.[114] The Derg gradually softened people up for the Emperor's removal, accusing him of amassing a private fortune, squandering the country's wealth, personal excesses and covering up the famine. When the Jonathan Dimbleby film was shown on 11th September in Ethiopia, intercut with scenes of the lavish lifestyles enjoyed by Selassie and his entourage while people starved to death, any remaining sympathy for him evaporated. The following day he was deposed, his land nationalised and he was put under house arrest. He died a prisoner less than a year later in August 1975. So without "firing a shot, the war of symbols had brought down the Lion of Judah" and, by staying its hand until it was confident of success, thereby allowing a power vacuum to develop, the Derg could claim not to be "usurping power, but ... saving the country from chaos".[115]

This chaos, and the further impoverishment Ethiopia had descended into, mirrored the Emperor's physical decline but, unlike his ordeal, the country's would continue long after his death. Nor was it to be a modern participatory democracy despite the apparent implications of the 'Ethiopia First' slogan. In fact this slogan could be used to justify coercion and suppression of peoples and individuals in the supposed national interest.[116] Selassie's successor as Head of State, along with sixty others from the old regime, was executed on the orders of the Derg in November 1974[117] - with, it is sometimes claimed, Mengistu personally involved in some of the high profile executions. Selassie may have been corrupt and corrupted by the office he occupied, by the expectations and powers attached to the role of Emperor, and he was certainly inept in his later years even before the task became utterly beyond him, but the country's repression was gentle and traditional under the Emperor compared to the bloodshed of the Mengistu regime. This should not be taken to mean, however, that the imperial subtlety made it appropriate or any less insidious.

Angola

One writer has described Angola as "a flash point in the Cold War rivalry" between the US and the USSR,[118] but this is but one ingredient in what was an extraordinarily complicated situation - especially by comparison to the unified approach of FRELIMO in Mozambique.

The first guerrilla organisation set up to fight for liberation from the Portuguese colonisers was the People's Movement for the

Liberation of Angola (MPLA) in 1956.[119] It was based in the capital city Luanda in the north-west of the country and led by Agostinho Neto from 1961. Seen as elitist and urban, and therefore dismissed by some as remote from rural peasants who comprised 85% of the Angolan population, the MPLA was soon challenged by a second nationalist organisation, the National Liberation Front of Angola (FNLA), which its leader Holden Roberto had set up originally in 1957 as the Union of the Peoples of Northern Angola (UPNA). Although the FNLA was made up in large measure from the Kikongo people of the north, many of them lived across the border with north Angola in Congo (Zaire) and, whether coincidentally or consequently, the FNLA had its headquarters in Zaire, drawing on support from that country's ruler President Mobutu, a relative of Holden Roberto by marriage.[120] The contrast between the two groups could hardly be sharper for the communist MPLA was seen as "cosmopolitan, socialist and integrated, the [FNLA as] provincial, entrepreneurial, anti-communist and ethnically homogeneous".[121]

In 1966 Jonas Savimbi fell out with the FNLA, for whom he had been a foreign minister, partly because they were not based in Angola itself, and set up the Union for the Total Independence of Angola (UNITA) in the south of the country among his own Ovimbundu people. UNITA's support came initially from China, but later from South Africa and the US.[122]

Each group rebelled against the Portuguese establishment which, according to Tvedten, countered by setting up a strategic hamlets programme in 1966 (similar to those in Malaya, Algeria and Vietnam previously and in Rhodesia subsequently) to isolate one million peasants from the guerrillas.[123] Like most of the other attempts it was counterproductive, leading to deteriorating conditions and increasing support for the rebels.[124] Ciment cites other misguided anti-guerrilla tactics the Portuguese had derived from the US, their NATO ally - as Newitt does too in relation to Mozambique where the Portuguese military commander endorsed the US resolve to "check the Communist advance in the world" and adopted their Vietnam tactics (such as overwhelming fire from helicopter gunships).[125]

But in addition the rebel organisations also fought each other for dominance, notably following the Portuguese revolution of April 1974, shortly after which Portugal indicated it would withdraw from its colonies (a process that France and Britain had started in the 1950s), and then in early 1975 when it became clear the three groups would be unable to reconcile their differences and share power after independence. This inter-group bloodshed can be traced back fourteen years to the start of the liberation war in 1961, when the MPLA and FNLA "would find themselves fighting each other as much as they did the Portuguese".[126] Similarly,

> ... just as charges of tribalism and communism haunted the FNLA and MPLA leadership respectively, so accusations of collaboration and opportunism dogged Savimbi. [It was reported that he had] agreed in the late 1960s to fight the MPLA and refrain from attacks on the Portuguese in exchange for UNITA authority in Ovimbuland.[127]

Consequently, rather than concentrating their resources on liberation and the post-colonial settlement, much was dissipated in fighting amongst themselves. This made the rapid Portuguese exit even more traumatic for the population than it would have been - and even a stable handover was always going to be painful, as well as in all likelihood chaotic.

Immediately after the coup in Portugal it looked as though the FNLA were poised to take power but the Portuguese brought the three groups together in January 1975 in the Alvor suburb of Lisbon. The agreement they signed, known as the Alvor Accords, declared that all three movements were the 'sole and legitimate representatives of the Angolan people' and that one representative from each should form a transitional government at independence on 11th November 1975, with elections to a national assembly to be held shortly before that date. But the celebrations of unity were short-lived, for by March the MPLA were fighting off the FNLA in Luanda and the FNLA were massacring MPLA recruits at a training camp.[128]

> With the situation growing increasingly fluid inside Angola, the superpowers and various African regimes began jockeying for influence. The CIA re-established its lapsed contacts with the FNLA, while China sent advisers and arms. The Soviet Union and Cuba, long-time supporters of the MPLA, began to airlift arms ... Mobutu

began setting up the infrastructure for an FNLA assault on northern Angola, while the South Africans sent out feelers to UNITA.[129]

The MPLA sought assistance from Katangese rebels deeply opposed to Mobutu and exiled in Angola, though this in turn justified Mobutu in sending more Zairian troops to reinforce the FNLA. The three rebel leaders met again in June in a further attempt to thrash out a joint solution and, while they agreed to continue working on a new constitution, their guerrilla armies were soon at war again. Just two weeks later the FNLA were threatening the MPLA stronghold in Luanda.

In August the CIA shipped arms to the FNLA, despite continuing scrutiny by Congress, and three ships left Cuba with 1500 troops to bolster the MPLA. On 10th November, the day before independence, "a combined army of Soviet-armed Cuban artillery units and MPLA infantry defeated the combined forces of Zairian artillery and FNLA infantry".[130] There was no formal independence ceremony on 11th November: Portugal lowered its flag at noon, declaring that it was up to the Angolan people to decide on how to exercise independence and left them to it, sailing off immediately. UNITA held a ceremony in Huambo in the southern part of the country while the FNLA and MPLA held separate ones in different parts of Luanda. Although the worst of the fighting had yet to come, it was the Cuban intervention that had put the MPLA in control of the parts of Luanda that mattered most, enabling them to evict the FNLA from the capital,[131] and was to reinforce their position elsewhere in the country subsequently, helped by the Clark Amendment halting US intervention and the withdrawal of South Africa, which had been helping Savimbi, into northern Namibia.[132] Hence, the MPLA leader Neto became the first President of the People's Republic of Angola.

Mozambique

Compared to the confused guerrilla situation in Angola, the Mozambique Liberation Front (FRELIMO) "was Mozambique's only serious guerrilla movement during the Portuguese era"[133] and came to power on independence in July 1975 under the leadership of Samora Machel. It had been formed in Dar es Salaam (the capital of Tanzania) in June 1962 when Presidents Nkrumah of Ghana and Nyerere of Tanzania persuaded three earlier resistance groups to come together.[134] Newitt described the pressure the two presidents exerted as "cajoled and bullied". At this stage the leadership of FRELIMO was mainly expatriate, with the first leader Eduardo Mondlane an official at the United Nations in New York. Branded unjustly and incorrectly as a US stooge for several years, and then murdered in 1969, Mondlane nevertheless contributed to the "remarkably cohesive and effective guerrilla movement" that FRELIMO became after his death.[135]

Before 1962 Portugal had taken some steps to free up their colonial regime, but this was for reasons other than preparing Mozambique for independence. On the contrary the motivation was to advance Portugal's status and position on the world stage. For example, as part of Salazar's campaign to shrug off the fascist associations from World War II (Portugal was officially neutral but a closet supporter of the Axis countries until 1943 when it switched allegiance as their prospects of victory foundered), the term 'colony' was dropped in favour of describing Mozambique as an 'Overseas Province'. When Portugal joined the United Nations in 1955, the UN Committee for Decolonization took an interest, "brushing aside [this] semantic device".[136] Joining the European Free Trade Area (EFTA) in 1960, and then obtaining EEC associate status in June 1970, required Portugal to concentrate its economy on Europe rather than its colonies and, in the latter case, to "dismantle the structure which had reserved colonial markets exclusively for Portuguese exports". Restrictions on foreign investment were also lifted and just as Mozambique looked increasingly to South Africa as its main export market so South Africa was the "principal source of external capital" in Mozambique by 1974.[137]

Although some industrialisation had been permitted since the late 1940s/1950s, Mozambique remained a largely peasant economy. This backwardness was mirrored in social and political under-development: for example, though there were 395 hospitals and a network of health care across the country by 1974, there were still only 400 doctors in total and no medical school.[138] Even more fundamentally, despite Portugal priding itself on being colour-blind the real system in force was a colour bar more subtle than apartheid. Africans were expected to join the labour market by, if not before, the time they completed fourth grade - whatever their age then. Machel had only been allowed to sit the fourth grade exams by becoming a Catholic in 1950 and attending a Catholic Mission School. He was told that he would have to join a seminary and train as a priest if he wanted to continue his education. Machel refused and became a nurse instead.[139] As Newitt describes the general position, "Educated Africans and Afro-Portuguese were required [in the modern economy], but continued to be marginalised in the state structure" with jobs taken by Portuguese immigrants or Indians.[140] Another insidious discrimination saw African farmers (including Machel's family) forced off their fertile land alongside the Limpopo in 1950 so that it could be handed to Portuguese settlers.[141] It should be no surprise therefore that FRELIMO "rebelled against ... the entire system of forced labour, repression of national consciousness and the institutionalised humiliation of Africans".[142]

The war of liberation continued for a decade from its modest start in September 1964 when twelve FRELIMO guerrillas attacked a Portuguese administrative post at Chai in the north of Mozambique, killing seven Portuguese.[143] The guerrillas had further successes in the north in 1965 before Portugal re-settled 250,000 people in 150 secure villages (aldeamentos) and exploited tribal, ethnic and religious differences to foster inter-rural rivalries. In 1969 a new military commander switched Portugal's policy from containment to offense to destroy FRELIMO bases and units in the north. This was followed by forty separate operations in 1970, deploying 35,000 troops and 100 helicopters and other aircraft. It was claimed that they destroyed 61 FRELIMO bases. The Portuguese government, alarmed by the casualties on their side, called a halt to further offensives and by 1973 more than half the security force within Mozambique was made up of locally- (and recently-) recruited black troops.[144]

But if Mozambique was polarised so was Portugal, with business demanding a political solution and the middle-classes asking questions of their regime. One in four of the Portuguese population had been conscripted and a million had served in Africa, but still the end of the war was not in sight. Discontent grew and "it simply required some act of will or vision to dismantle the now hollow and expensive structure".[145] After the Portugal coup in April

1974 and the removal of Caetano, who had replaced his long-time colleague Salazar when the latter suffered a stroke in 1968, General Spinola had been installed as leader. However, Spinola's conservatism was at odds with the views of the officers who had led the coup and who were determined to see a complete transfer of power to FRELIMO.[146] For them "a radical structure in Africa was seen as essential for a radical regime in Portugal". They removed Spinola on 9th July and the Portuguese army in Mozambique offered no opposition or resistance, though some right-wing settlers did, and the Lusaka Accord of 7th September 1974 agreed independence within nine months without elections. Both parties were keen to keep the transition period brief so that right-wing opposition forces had no chance to re-group. The interim government ahead of independence would be led by Chissano, subsequently President of Mozambique after Machel's death in a plane crash in October 1986.[147]

There had been a war of liberation from Portugal in the 1960s, but unlike Angola there was no war of independence.

> FRELIMO … had no serious political rivals [and] no South African invasion. … FRELIMO's long-term commitment to in-country political and social organising during the war of liberation, helped minimise the urban intellectual - rural peasantry gap that plagued the MPLA and helped to create a culture of shared sacrifice among the FRELIMO leadership.[148]

The handover of power to FRELIMO in July 1975 (known as the Frelimo party, in lower-case, once in government) was not only planned but peaceful. Yet a year later a second rebel group RENAMO was set up by Rhodesia's Central Intelligence Organisation (the one headed by Ken Flower) to fight Frelimo and their antagonism to the Rhodesian regime as evident in their "strict application of international sanctions".[149] This conflict lasted initially to 1992 and then broke out again for a further three years in 2013. Talks have been taking place between the Mozambique government and RENAMO since 2016 and a solution was reached in August 2019, ahead of a visit by Pope Francis.[150] It remains to be seen whether it will last.

After independence, according to Newitt, the Frelimo government continued to face the key economic question that had dogged Portugal previously:

> How does a relatively poor and undeveloped country develop itself when the market place for labour, consumer goods and capital is dominated by a much bigger and relatively more developed neighbouring economy?,

in this case South Africa.[151] Mozambique did not have the natural resources of Angola, though it did have comparative social and political stability. Nevertheless, the question is yet to be fully resolved.

Vietnam

The North Vietnamese communists exhibited several of the characteristics attributed by Ciment to FRELIMO; that is to say, leadership that was intelligent and experienced, not to say inspired, an ideology shared by both the intellectuals and the peasants, and a commitment to a war of liberation. In North Vietnam's case this was waged first against the French and then the US, regardless of personal and community sacrifice. South Vietnam by contrast, Gabriel Kolko argues, showed a "profound dependency" on the US for every detail of men, materials, etc. This in turn resulted in "a passive colonial mentality".[152] Nguyen van Thieu had been President since June 1967, and his administration, like that of Nixon's, was corrupt, though in South Vietnam's case financially as well as morally so. Indeed it was the endemic and systematic financial corruption that kept Thieu in power, just as it was American aid and US military requirements (including direct employment of 145,000 South Vietnamese in 1969) that concealed the chasms at the heart of the country's economy. For Kolko, South Vietnam

> ... fell into a fatal syndrome after 1972 in which its military ambitions gravely undermined its economy, economic failures eroded its already narrow political support, and economic and political trends quickly sapped its military structure.[153]

1974 appeared to be a quiet year in Vietnam but it would become clear by the start of the next that this had been deceptive. The Paris ceasefire signed by Henry Kissinger and Le Duc Tho had come into effect on 28 January 1973, but both Nixon and Thieu assumed it to be no more than a pause. So, while the last American troops left Vietnam shortly afterwards,[154] and combat troops had left in August 1972,[155] Nixon was threatening to revive the air offensive against Hanoi. This galvanised the US Senate to vote overwhelmingly "to cut off funds for any form of US combat anywhere in Indochina", a law that came into effect mid-August 1973 after Nixon had first used the Presidential veto before backing down.[156] The US strategy of détente with the USSR crumbled soon afterwards.

Thieu's policy after Paris was to hold and expand territory, though this would make it more vulnerable to Communist attack if (or, more probably, when) the ceasefire categorically ended. To this was added controls over people's movements and trade, both violations of the Paris agreement, and an army that was too large and poorly paid survived only by looting villages and stealing from peasants, thereby increasing their dissatisfaction with Thieu's regime.[157]

North Vietnam, meanwhile, had taken note of the warnings from their paymasters in China and the USSR "not to precipitate a crisis in the south, and ... that they would not provide arms for any escalation". What both Moscow and Peking assured North Vietnam they would do, however, was give the country "enough to protect and consolidate its power".[158] By avoiding combat the North was recovering and re-arming, while the South was over-extending its depleted resources into new areas. Strategically, the North was biding its time as Thieu became politically and economically weaker, with the added benefit as it turned out of the US increasingly traumatised by Watergate, frozen diplomatically as well as militarily.[159]

Thieu and his military commanders had always assumed that, in the final analysis, the US would save South Vietnam and his regime. But when the Communist offensive came in early 1975 this hope proved wildly misplaced. From the fall of Hue and the abandonment of the Danang air base, both at the end of March, to the unconditional surrender on 30th April, the capitulation was both swift and abject. Thieu himself had resigned on 21st April, the same day Saigon had been surrounded by North Vietnamese troops, and he fled the country four days later. On 23rd April President Ford, Nixon's replacement, had announced that as far as the US was concerned, "the Vietnam War is finished". In chaotic scenes captured on television the last Americans left on 30th April, evacuated from the roof of the American embassy by helicopters that came in fast and scurried out as quickly. The humiliation was complete.

5.   AGAINST THE ODDS: THE US ILLUSION EXPOSED

Losing the Vietnam war dealt a hammer blow to belief in the US, both its own assurance that it was the super-power in excelsis that had already dominated the world for thirty years since being forced to shrug off its global isolation in 1941 and the understanding of many other countries around the world that, when push came to shove, it was the US that they could rely on or, if they were on the other side, had to fear. The internal and external view previously was that this domination would continue but events in Vietnam had shown it to be illusory, a mirage that was unsustainable when a country of 203 million (in 1970) at the cutting edge of technology, particularly military technology, had been humbled by a peasant population one-tenth its size.[160] The doctrine that had previously prevailed of 'might is right' had come up against a people that, fighting for its beliefs, was more determined and could flex but would not be pushed around, let alone be a push-over. Military muscle had proved no match for a secular ideology that, absorbed from childhood, was ingrained and had the same status for its adherents as religious faith does for its disciples.

In a very real sense this dissolving US omnipotence was simply the culmination on the international stage of domestic fracturing that had been building through the 1960s. There are several examples but to pick just three: the youth protests against the Vietnam war and their violent suppression in the second half of the 1960s, the 1967 race riots and Daniel Ellsberg's unauthorised publication of the Pentagon Papers in the *New York Times* (and other newspapers) in June 1971.[161]

There were race riots throughout the decade, for example in 1965 in Watts and in 1968 after the assassination of Martin Luther King, but in 1967 there were more than 150 in cities as varied as Newark, Detroit, Chicago and Los Angeles. They sparked across the country from coast to coast and for a number of reasons, but the excessive use of police force, extending in some instances to police brutality, was the universal response.

The Pentagon Papers had been commissioned by Robert McNamara, the Defense Secretary in 1967, to set out the history of US involvement in south-east Asia. Ellsberg had been one of the authors and compiling the dossier had added to his disillusionment with the Vietnam war, not least because the documentation laid bare the lies that successive administrations (particularly the Lyndon Johnson one) had told in order to justify US actions.

It might be observed that the establishment in each instance reacted extremely, often with the truncheon and the gun or where, as with the *New York Times*, they had to be more cautious and circumspect, with the injunction and the lawsuit. In each instance it was as if the authorities were not only wounded but felt themselves cornered and were lashing out viciously in an attempt to subdue opposition and dissent. This indiscriminate response is often an indication of weakness not strength, but it is also a learned behaviour that, if effective on enough occasions, is reinforced as the preferred choice. It proved as ineffective in addressing the causes of the riots and the student protests as it did in censoring the newspapers and bludgeoning the North Vietnamese to defeat.

Yet these events might also be thought to be triumphs as well as humiliations, in that each depended on one group standing up for its rights and beliefs in the face of a bureaucracy that could easily crush them. There was to be another spectacular and singular event in 1974 that would colour the view other countries around the world took of the US, and again such views would be polarised. On the one hand when the pinnacle of the State resigned over Watergate in August, a corrupt and venal Richard Nixon had been undone by a hubris and ego that led him to act as if the President was above the law. Or, as Louis Liebovich describes it, "Watergate was not about a break-in; it was about a mindset and that mindset had now been revealed publicly." Liebovich emphasised this point in his analysis:

> It was not so much the nature of the underhanded malfeasance that led to the administration's destruction as it was the underlying convictions that justified them. ... The President and his staff were prisoners to both a paranoid ideology and a cloistered existence.[162]

On the other hand Nixon had been exposed by a newspaper making full use of the moral authority and permission that the constitution gave the press. The strength of the US constitution had been pitted against the person supposed to embody it, but whose actions had undermined it. Nor, it should be added, had the

Washington Post the safety in numbers that the *New York Times* had relied on in releasing the Pentagon Papers. This makes the determination of the editor Ben Bradlee and his staff, and that of the owner Katharine (Kay) Graham, to withstand the pressure from the administration and keep the story alive even more courageous.[163] 'Right is might' in effect, the belief that succoured the Vietnamese and informed the course they adopted - as the civil rights movement also displayed, though it would take longer for it to have any appreciable effect.

Liebovich identifies the publication of the Pentagon Papers, four months after the equally revealing CBS television documentary 'Selling of the Pentagon', as the catalyst that prompted the Nixon White House to start taping all conversations. Liebovich asserts that some previous presidents had kept a taped record of selected discussions, but it was the all-encompassing nature of the Nixon programme that shows a president who not only found these disclosures toxic but interpreted them as a hostile media laying siege to the White House and his administration.[164] The irony is that the Pentagon Papers were about earlier presidential regimes and the CBS documentary was only tangentially about Nixon. Nevertheless, the White House attitude thereafter was 'anything goes' in order to ensure Nixon was re-elected in 1972.[165]

Even in the first eighteen months after taking office Nixon, and his chief of staff HR Haldeman, had engaged in measures, including phone tapping, to counter individual journalists whose coverage they found hostile.[166] Rather than different views being interpreted as indicative of a healthy democracy, they were seen as the outpourings of a malevolent fourth estate and of individual practitioners within it. Given this belief system, Nixon and Haldeman may even have justified their descent to covert surveillance as the appropriate response in the circumstances. This personalisation of the conflict was taken further in March 1970 when leaks from White House staffers were first outlawed and then, when they continued, Haldeman's staff called in 'plumbers' to fix the leaks and punish the leakers.[167] It was then only a short step across the moral threshold to find out what Nixon's Democratic opponents in the presidential election were up to in their Watergate building headquarters. Here too 'plumbers' set phone taps but the burglary was carried out so ineptly that it was discovered even before the plumbers left the building.

Nixon would almost certainly have won the 1972 election anyway for the likeliest and strongest Democratic opponent Senator Edmund Muskie had collapsed tearfully during the campaign, the racist Governor of Alabama George Wallace had been shot and the eventual nominee George McGovern was judged too liberal. In addition, a chaotic Democratic Party convention in July 1972, the month after the Watergate burglary, included McGovern's acceptance speech at 3am (which few of the electorate saw or heard) and was followed by McGovern's nominee as vice-president, Thomas Eagleton, withdrawing after ten days. A number of possible replacements refused until an obscure member of the Kennedy clan, Sargent Shriver, eventually accepted. To the average American elector, therefore, McGovern appeared to be incompetent as well as "a dangerous radical" and unfit to be president. By comparison, the incumbent was working to end America's involvement in Vietnam, had re-opened relations with China, was pursuing détente with the Soviet Union and was presiding over an improving economy.[168] Nixon seemed to offer the stability at home for which America was hankering after the tumultuous 1960s, as well as optimism about the country's international future in a nuclear age. Not surprisingly, his victory was overwhelming, winning over 60% of the popular vote and all but two of the fifty-one states.

From this high point, when Nixon was seen as "a highly successful politician", matters went downhill and a year later at the end of 1973 he was judged "a beaten man who was marking time until his resignation".[169]

The Watergate burglary had taken place on 17th June 1972[170] and Nixon first discussed it on tape three days later when he was back in the White House after a holiday. By October it was clear to the *Washington Post* that it was not an isolated incident but part of an overall dirty tricks campaign by the White House, at which point the paper's editors added their interest to that of their reporters Bob Woodward and Carl Bernstein.[171] By February 1973 the Senate had started its own inquiry under Senator Sam Ervin, adding a third investigation to the court trial of the burglars overseen by Judge Sirica and that of the *Washington Post*. A number of key officials in the administration, Nixon's chief of staff HR Haldeman, his domestic adviser John Ehrlichman, White House counsel John Dean and the Attorney-General Richard Kleindeinst, in effect Nixon's inner circle, resigned at the end of April 1973 but, rather than enabling Nixon to move on, this made people and the press more interested in the unfolding story. Nixon appeared on television that night, absolving himself of any blame and promising justice.[172]

Ervin's Senate Committee hearings started on 17th May and ran to 7th August, thirty-seven days of testimony in all, 237 hours of which were televised. The highlights were Dean's appearance over five days at the end of June, exposing the extent of the cover-up and claiming that Nixon had known for nine months since he was told the details the previous September (i.e., before the presidential election), and that of Haldeman's aide Alexander Butterfield on 16th July 1973 who revealed that "Nixon had been taping most of his conversations for more than two years".[173] This admission exploded like a grenade for it had been known previously to only a handful of people and was a revelation to the Senate Committee. Getting Nixon to release the tapes now became the priority.

Nixon argued that 'executive privilege' meant he did not have to provide them, a stance he tried to maintain in one form or another until the US Supreme Court voted 8-0 in July 1974 endorsing Judge Sirica's ruling at the end of May that year demanding sixty-four of them. They included one tape from 23rd June 1972, less than a week after the Watergate break-in, in which Nixon had ordered that the CIA be used to block the investigation the FBI had already started. This was not the only 'smoking gun' in the tapes but, if released, could be enough on its own to blow Nixon's defence out of the water.

Meanwhile the economy had deteriorated and all the country's international business had ground to a halt. As Garthoff puts it, the "exercise of power [had been] sharply constrained, part of the price of fighting for the presidency" for Nixon could not afford to antagonise either his remaining supporters or his enemies.[174] The vice-president Spiro Agnew had resigned on 6th October 1973[175] over income tax evasion and was replaced by Gerald Ford. Other countries revelled in America's growing discomfort, using it for their own ends or to justify inaction, such as that which overtook the US-USSR discussions on détente or stayed American intervention in Cyprus, with "Nixon wholly estranged from such policy matters" by the time of the Turkish invasion.[176] As one Soviet observer put it subsequently, why should any adversary of the US rely on 'gentleman's promises' when even American people couldn't "rely on [their] President's word of honour".[177]

At the end of July 1974 the House Judiciary Committee laid three articles of impeachment for debate on 19th August. These were that Nixon had obstructed justice, abused his power as president and impeached himself by not providing the tapes requested by the Committee. Nixon did then release the CIA tape from June 1972 on 5th August claiming that it "sounded much worse [than was] meant".[178] He resigned three days later to take effect from noon on the next day 9th August, preferring the humiliation of resignation to the indignity of impeachment. The new President Gerald Ford sought to draw a line under Watergate, "to end the national trauma", by pardoning Nixon on 8th September.[179] This might have been an "act of courage", as Liebovich puts it, but it was inept and undercut the reputation for probity that Ford had accrued over his twenty-five years in Congress. Ford was the first of three presidents over the next eighteen years (Jimmy Carter and George Bush were the others) who were not re-elected for a second term.

In a speech to the Senate Foreign Relations Committee in September 1974 Kissinger had maintained that the new Ford administration would pursue the same 1972 trade accords and process of détente with the Soviet Union as had the Nixon one, but this never produced any tangible results.[180] Kissinger's self-belief and his assumption of intellectual infallibility were no longer enough to persuade others on its own, and the national swagger and assumption of superiority that previously would have convinced or coerced others to follow the US line had been undermined.

6. STATE PREROGATIVE: REPRESSION AT HOME AND DÉTENTE ABROAD - THE SOVIET UNION AND THE EASTERN BLOC

The apparent contradiction between the Soviet Union seeking superpower détente while suppressing neighbouring countries in the Eastern bloc that stepped out of line and repressing those of its citizens who questioned the regime has been pointed out by many commentators. Daniel Möckli, for example, has asked whether repression at home could conceivably be compatible with détente abroad.[181] Alexander Solzhenitsyn, the Nobel laureate for literature in 1970, had been thrown out of the Soviet Union in February 1974 and little more than a year later was berating a Washington audience for the concessions the West had made to the USSR in the thirty years since the end of the Second World War. In Solzhenitsyn's view "During these thirty years, more was surrendered to totalitarianism than any defeated country has ever surrendered after any war in history," indicating to the USSR that the West was more likely to accede to its requests than stand firm.[182] The Yalta conference had confirmed the occupation of the Baltic states, "almost nothing was done to protect eastern Europe, and seven or eight more countries were surrendered".[183]

Solzhenitsyn's speech included the example of Raoul Wallenberg, a Swedish citizen who, part of a US-funded mission, saved Budapest's Jews from the Nazis in 1944 but disappeared himself into the Soviet prison system the following year. Solzhenitsyn said Wallenberg was still there in 1975 and his fate remains unknown today, though his relatives are again demanding the Swedish government find out what happened to him.[184]

Solzhenitsyn's expulsion had long been anticipated for, while the Soviet Union

chokes over Solzhenitsyn and Sakharov, the other leading dissident, as the US chokes over Watergate ... more complex and more flexible ... systems, like Britain and France could absorb both. ...
To be fair to the Russian Establishment, they are being attacked on basic principles, not just on a particular series of persecutions under a particular leader now dead.[185]

The Soviet state would argue that it was acting entirely consistently in protecting the communist system and its citizens. Capping the spend on arms and agreeing trade arrangements would strengthen the economic and employment performance of the USSR, as well as its security, whereas allowing dissident voices to go unchallenged might fracture and undermine the political system and the communist ideology that underpinned it. This is how any totalitarian state would justify censorship and even the incarceration of political prisoners. Whether it could also rationalise the inhumanity of labour camps, which Solzhenitsyn termed the 'Gulag Archipelago', and the abuse of psychiatry to silence critics, might be more problematic.[186] Denial of such practices was the default position - even when the Canadian Psychiatric Association became the first to condemn the confinement in mental hospitals of healthy people with non-conformist political views.[187]

Similarly, permitting Jewish people to emigrate and see for themselves might convince them that capitalism was a preferable system to the Soviet one, an argument the USSR was not about to concede. Some Jewish people might seek to move abroad because of belief in Israel as the spiritual homeland, or to re-unify families, but arbitrary and unexplained refusals by the USSR authorities simply added to the political and economic discrimination that many sought to escape.[188]

In 1970 the population of the Soviet Union at 241 million was almost a fifth larger than that of the USA,[189] with their urban populations defined differently: America as those living in a settlement over 2500 people, the USSR by type of activity. On this basis 43% of the USSR population were classified as rural in that they were engaged in agriculture, whereas only a quarter of the USA's were so described in that they lived in settlements smaller than 2500 people. The most obvious differences though were in age and sex: in both countries about 38% of the population were under 20, but in the USA almost 10% were 65 or older against less than 8% in the USSR. This reflects in particular the huge number of adult Soviet deaths during the Second World War - though other factors, such as harsher living conditions and the country's generally lower standard of health care, may have played some part. The impact of the Second World War is also evident in the figures for females: they comprised nearly 54% of the overall population in the USSR but 69% of those aged 65 or older, whereas the USA figures were 51% and 58% respectively. Even though the Second World War had been over for nearly thirty years its legacy in the USSR was still apparent and was bound to have an impact on the Soviet approach to international relations. Had there not been pressures in the other direction as well, its approach might have been even more belligerent and aggressive than in fact it was.

The Soviet sphere of influence in Eastern Europe had been established shortly after WWII ended, initially comprising eight countries, though Yugoslavia had always been semi-detached and under Marshal Tito, who had driven the Nazis out without any assistance from the Soviet Union, it split from Moscow in 1948/49. Albania supported China rather than the USSR in the 1960 schism over approaches to communism, becoming China's only European ally and the most isolated country in Europe under the regime of Enver Hoxha. This left six countries as Soviet satellites in the Eastern bloc: Poland, Hungary, Czechoslovakia, East Germany (the German Democratic Republic or GDR), and in the south of Europe Bulgaria and Romania. They provided the Soviet Union with a "defensive buffer zone" against the West and under Stalin, it has been argued, a way of keeping Western Europe "politically and even militarily intimidated and ... off balance".[190] The Baltic States of Estonia, Latvia and Lithuania had been re-absorbed into the USSR in 1940 and Berlin had a special status, reflecting the position at the end of WWII.

Willy Brandt had started West Germany's (Federal Republic of Germany or FRG's) policy of *Ostpolitik* in 1966 when he was Foreign Minister in the 'grand coalition' led by the CDU/CSU in which his party (the SPD) was the junior partner. The essence of this approach to relations with Eastern Europe and the Soviet Union was normalisation as a condition for, rather than consequence of, détente. Under the policy, diplomatic relations were first established with Romania and Yugoslavia from 1967 and 1968 respectively. The GDR objected strongly to the establishment of diplomatic relations with Romania for a 1966 declaration was supposed to have bound

all Warsaw Pact states. It had made clear that diplomatic relations could not be entered into with Bonn before the latter had recognised the GDR in international law. Ulbricht [then leader of the GDR] reacted furiously and belaboured the Romanians ..., but the Romanians accused the GDR of interfering in their internal affairs. For a while it looked as if other East European states would follow suit, the bait being improved economic relations.[191]

That they did not was due to a subsequent meeting of European communist parties which

... reiterated the GDR's view that diplomatic relations with Bonn should follow the normalisation of relations between the two German states. [Nevertheless,] This whole episode illustrates the leeway which East European states enjoyed at this time. The GDR needed the backing of the USSR to ensure that its interests took precedence over those of the other East European states.[192]

In 1969 Brandt became FRG Chancellor and made relations with East Germany a priority. Since the Berlin Wall had been built in 1961, families had been separated and people living in the West, not just in Berlin, had no guarantee of access even to West Berlin. Brandt's immediate aim was to establish a practical solution that would reduce the "human problems" and, by recognising the border with the GDR, would begin to overcome it. A treaty was signed with Moscow in August 1970, winning Brandt the Nobel Peace Prize, and a Quadripartite Agreement on Berlin was concluded in 1971.[193] The latter confirmed West Berlin's ties to the FRG and guaranteed western access to West Berlin; also, West Berliners were able to visit the East (both Berlin and the GDR as a whole) for the first time since 1961. In December 1972 the FRG and GDR signed a Treaty setting out the Basis of their Relations. It had been preceded by FRG normalising its diplomatic relations with Poland two years earlier and was followed by similar agreements with Czechoslovakia, Bulgaria and Hungary at the end of 1973.[194]

On the face of it, therefore, *Ostpolitik* had regularised FRG's relations with Eastern Europe in the space of seven years. Although the Soviet Union might be nervous about the FRG's relationship with countries such as Poland, they must have been most concerned about the links with East Germany, even suspecting the FRG's ultimate motive was reunification.[195] In addition, the prospect of a resurgent Germany must have summoned up the horrors the

The strapline translates as
"... how so? They don't exist so nothing can have happened!"
Die Mauerphilosophie 23 March 1968
© Ernst Maria Lang

USSR and Poland, in particular, had suffered in the Second World War. Partly for this reason problems began in 1973 on implementing the Quadripartite Agreement and Basic Treaty, though *Ostpolitik* had also raised concerns among the FRG's Western allies. It "had defused some essential points of contention between East and West and in that sense had brought more stability to the Cold War international system", but had also suggested the FRG might pursue a unilateral course of rapprochement rather than as part of overall East-West relations.[196] Then the economic crisis of October 1973 changed FRG priorities in any case.[197]

Leonid Brezhnev (1906-1982) had replaced Nikita Khrushchev in October 1964 as leader of the Communist Party in the Soviet Union while his colleague Alexei Kosygin became head of the USSR government. Coincidentally, this change had occurred on the same day that Harold Wilson won the UK election.[198] The alleged reason Khrushchev was ousted was his bad health but in reality he was dumped as First Secretary of the Communist Party of the Soviet Union and Chairman of the USSR Council of Ministers because of his arbitrary approach to leadership that had alienated virtually all his previous supporters, as well as his risky approach to policy formulation and policy failures abroad. In addition, he had tried to resolve the economic problems left by his predecessor Stalin too quickly and "his conduct of foreign affairs and agricultural development" destabilised the Soviet Union's view of its place in the world and ended the optimism which at first had accompanied Khrushchev's elevation to power.[199]

In contrast to the upheavals of the Stalin and Khrushchev years, Brezhnev preferred stability, though later this came to be portrayed as stagnation as the "conservative, incremental biases of the [policy-making] system were no longer countered by the ambitions of a strong leader".[200] In his first years in office, Brezhnev's leadership was characterised, particularly in comparison to the one-person cults of Stalin and Khrushchev, as consultative and consensual. In the view of some commentators, this had begun to change by 1967/68 when alternative power centres had either been removed or had disappeared and Brezhnev had less need to keep others on board. Others argue that this early approach lasted throughout Brezhnev's first decade before his health began to deteriorate in 1974.[201] But in any event he was unchallenged by the latter year and became increasingly autocratic as well as insecure.

In 1968, largely in response to the 'Prague spring' in Czechoslovakia and to justify the subsequent invasion by Warsaw Pact forces, Brezhnev had laid out what later came to be known as the Brezhnev Doctrine. This asserted that

> ... the interests of the socialist commonwealth transcended that of individual socialist states and that socialist states were duty-bound to come to the aid of socialism wherever it was threatened.[202]

It was akin to the rationale of 'collective defence' which had led to the formation of NATO in 1949, though it enlarged on the mutual responsibilities agreed in the Warsaw Pact of 1955.[203] In so doing

...it bound all the states more closely together - the exception being Romania - and it ensured tighter control for Moscow, especially in foreign policy. Defensive solidarity vis-à-vis the West became the order of the day.[204]

An illustration of the Brezhnev Doctrine in practice was provided elsewhere by the Soviet Union's support for the Cuban revolution, a point emphasised by Fidel Castro when Brezhnev visited the island in January 1974. Not only had the Soviet Union's help enabled Cuba to cope with the US economic blockade, but the USSR had not sought anything in return, for as Castro put it in his welcome speech,

> The Soviet Union - a Socialist and deeply internationalistic nation - does not own in our homeland a single mine, business, or public service. It has not invested a single cent in Cuba expecting profit.

In return Brezhnev promised "Revolutionary Cuba has never been and will never be alone".[205]

Czechoslovakia was a tipping point, not only in the deployment of Warsaw Pact forces (other than those of Romania) to crush reforms that threatened the communist project, but in encouraging dissidents within the Soviet Union to protest. Their hopes had been raised by the freedoms opening up in Czechoslovakia and, rather than being cowed by the military action, they re-doubled their efforts to make their voices heard. The nuclear physicist Andrei Sakharov, previously a pillar of the scientific community, had first published 'Progress, Co-existence and Intellectual Freedom' in Moscow in May 1968 at the height of the 'Prague spring' but it came to the West's attention after the reforms had been reversed in August. Even though Solzhenitsyn did not agree with all Sakharov's views, he applauded the enthusiasm with which he had expressed them.[206] The genie was out of the bottle.

The US and USSR met in June 1974 to continue their strategic arms limitation talks, intending that increased détente would lead to improved trade relations, but progress was hampered by the growing spectre of Watergate that, two months before his resignation, disabled Nixon from any policy initiatives.[207] In addition Pentagon hawks, including the US Secretary of Defense, did not believe in further détente and sought to undermine the SALT talks and hence the US President. A weakened Nixon was unable to fire him.[208] Others, such as Senator Henry Jackson, attacked normalisation of trade relations with the USSR, opposing 'most favoured nation' status (i.e., the lowest tariffs) for the USSR and any extended lines of credit or enhanced lending (above $300m) to them. If such concessions were to be granted, Senator Jackson argued, they should be linked to increased Jewish emigration and more enlightened handling of political dissidents in the USSR. To underline the strength of his objections Senator Jackson pointedly visited China while the talks were being held in Moscow, a snub that the Soviet press picked up.[209] Meanwhile, to make the point that he had not been sidelined or gone away, Sakharov had begun a hunger strike on the second day of the conference.[210]

Even without Watergate these dissident voices in the US might have been enough to scupper the talks - and they were echoed by similar, if more muted, anxieties in the USSR where the military-defence establishment was just as sceptical of political manoeuvres and equally influential.

Although it had no immediate impact for it took two years to reach agreement, which even then had no legal force, the Helsinki Conference on Security Co-operation in Europe (CSCE) initiated by the Soviet Union in 1974 was to prove hugely significant in the long-term. The CSCE involved all European states (other than Albania), as well as the US and Canada, and the Helsinki Final Act as it became known was signed by 35 countries in July 1975. Tompson describes this as the high point of détente, with agreement in three key areas (or "baskets" in CSCE terminology). The first of these, known as the security dimension, confirmed post-war borders and non-intervention in the affairs of other states, so while the latter is hard to square with the Brezhnev doctrine the former had long been an objective of the Soviet Union.[211] The second, the economic dimension, covered economic, scientific, technological and environmental co-operation, as well as migrant labor, vocational training and the promotion of tourism. The third "human dimension" covered human rights or, as the OSCE website describes it today, "co-operation in humanitarian and other fields: freer movement of people; human contacts, including family reunification and visits; freedom of information, including working conditions for journalists; and cultural and educational exchanges".[212] At first sight this might appear to be a major concession by the Soviet Union for it encouraged increased emigration and was certainly interpreted as legitimising internal dissent, becoming a manifesto for Eastern European dissidents,[213] yet it was in theory no more extensive than the UN Convention on Human Rights that the USSR had signed in 1973.[214] However, the Soviet Union's response exposed the hypocrisy, with Helsinki Watch Groups set up in Moscow, Kiev, Vilnius, Tbilisi and Yerevan to monitor the reality of their limited and dismissive engagement. As Valery Chalidze, who had founded the Moscow Committee for Human Rights in 1970 along with Sakharov, put it:

> On the one hand a state makes commitments to guarantee human rights on its own territory, while on the other hand it tells those to whom the commitment was made that securing human rights is exclusively its internal affair.[215]

This view is the same as that adopted by one recent commentator, who argues that, because human rights are subordinate to state sovereignty in international law, the UN Declaration is therefore unenforceable.[216] However, it would be a very strange situation indeed if this was legitimately the case, for it would mean that the world organisation the supra-national UN was subordinate to the legal arrangements within individual member countries as well as between them.

Chalidze had been forced into exile in 1972, his passport cancelled while he was on a visit to the US, and by 1974 he had been joined by many others, such as the cellist Rostropovich and the poet Brodsky, both of whom had opted for expulsion rather than imprisonment. The rationale, according to Rubenstein, was that the Soviet Union government hoped that "The emigration of well-known figures … would camouflage increased repression inside the country".[217] It did not, of course, and Brezhnev's successors Andropov and Chernenko sought to keep the lid on the pressure cooker. It would be 1985 before Gorbachev became President of the USSR, ushering in an era of greater openness (glasnost) and restructuring (perestroika) to address the harsh economic reality that his three predecessors had failed to tackle.

7. POLITICAL CHANGE IN WESTERN EUROPE: GREECE, FRANCE, WEST GERMANY AND PORTUGAL

The pattern of electoral support for Left parties in fourteen European countries during the 1970s is set out in Donald Sassoon's 'One Hundred Years of Socialism'.[218] Seven of these countries are covered in some detail in this book (those above the bold line in Table 2 below), while the other seven are mentioned only in passing. Table 2 has been derived from the information provided by Sassoon (as has the graph of average electoral support during the 1970s shown on p87, where the SPÖ, Austria's party of the Left had the highest electoral support on average during the 1970s).

Country	1970s			
	Average (%)	Low (%)	High (%)	Pattern[219]
Austria	50.0	48.4	51.0	steady
France	22.1	19.2	25.0	up
Greece	19.5	13.6	25.3	up
Italy	30.7	27.2	34.4	up/down
Portugal	35.4	28.9	40.7	decreasing
UK	39.8	37.0	43.1	decreasing
West Germany	44.2	42.6	45.8	steady
Belgium	26.4	25.4	27.2	steady
Denmark	33.6	25.6	38.3	down/up
Finland	24.5	23.4	25.8	steady
Holland	28.6	24.6	33.8	increasing
Norway	38.8	35.3	42.3	up
Spain	30.4	30.3	30.5	steady
Sweden	43.7	42.7	45.3	steady

Table 2: Highs and lows of percentage share of the vote for parties of the Left in the 1970s[220]

In this decade, the Austrian and West German parties of the Left (SPÖ and SPD respectively) were both the strongest and the most stable. Both were in government throughout this period. There were four Austrian general elections during these years, and three West German ones, and each party's share of the vote varied by no more than three percentage points throughout. Only the Left party in Sweden was anything like as strong and stable (though those in

Norway and Holland improved their share of the vote over the decade). Olof Palme's Social Democrats were in government in Sweden for the first half of the 1970s.

Support went up over the decade for the Socialist parties in France and Greece, and both became even stronger during the 1980s, but noticeably declined for the Labour Party in the UK and the Socialists in Portugal. The Labour Party's share of the vote reduced further in the 1980s, as did that of the Portuguese Socialists - apart from a brief but major recovery in 1983. Nevertheless, Soares' Socialists received a sufficient share of the vote themselves, and were able to form coalitions with other parties, to ensure Soares became Prime Minister in both 1976 and 1983. By contrast the UK Labour Party was in government only for the five years 1974-1979. In Italy the Communist Party was a special case. It declined after 1976 and Italy's political parties became increasingly fragmented in the 1980s.

In April 1975 just before he was due to lead a Socialist delegation to Moscow, the future French president Francois Mitterand protested about Solzhenitsyn's banishment, Rostropovich's exile, and the right of Soviet Jews to emigrate. He also berated the Portuguese Communists, "the last Stalinists in Western Europe" he called them, "for sending party thugs to wreck the newspaper offices of their rival, Mario Soares' Socialist Party, in Lisbon".[221] (The Italian Communist leader Enrico Berlinguer also distanced himself from them.)[222] The USSR responded by cancelling the visit but uproar in the French press led to the Soviet Union backing down. Coming at the same time as the Helsinki agreement was close to signature, the Soviet Union may have been mindful of their audience in Western Europe.

Mitterand had lost to Valery Giscard d'Estaing in the May 1974 French presidential election, called after Georges Pompidou had died in office less than five years into his seven year term.[223] However, Mitterand would beat Giscard in the subsequent presidential election in 1981 going on to serve two full terms to 1995.

This was but one example of extensive political changes, at least in leadership personnel, across Europe in 1974. And the new leadership in many of these countries, and the existing one in Austria, was to prove critical in 1974.

Giscard d'Estaing initially appointed Jacques Chirac as his Prime Minister, though two years later in the face of economic downturn he turned to the economist Raymond Barre, while another presidential death, this time in Austria, led to the election there of Rudolf Kirchschläger. But whereas the French president was the executive head of state, the Austrian post was largely ceremonial and it was the Chancellor Bruno Kreisky, then only four years into a premiership that would last until 1983, who exercised the political authority. In Spain General Franco's ill-health meant that he temporarily handed over to his eventual replacement as head of state Juan Carlos, later King after Franco died in November 1975. The transfer of power in West Germany might have been more turbulent when Willy Brandt resigned as Chancellor after one of his aides had been arrested as an East German spy, but there was a subdued, and to all intents seamless, transition as his party colleague and Finance Minister Helmut Schmidt replaced him. Portugal might also have been very different but the Salazar/Caetano regime was overthrown without bloodshed in April and the first President, Spinola, was succeeded by another general Costa Gomes at the end of September. In Greece the chiefs of the armed forces invited the exiled Constantine Karamanlis to return to form a government of national unity. In Italy there were neo-fascist demonstrations and the first Red Brigade murders.[224] In Israel, closely linked to Western Europe, Golda Meir resigned as Prime Minister and Yitzhak Rabin took over.

There were elections in Belgium, Iceland and Luxembourg, as well as the two in the UK already referred to in Chapter 2. In Belgium the Socialists were the largest party but Leo Tindemans of the right-wing Christian Democrats led a coalition government. Only in the Scandinavian countries was there no political change in Western Europe in 1974.

Ian Kershaw asserts that the three authoritarian regimes of Portugal, Greece and Spain collapsed within a few months of each other in 1974 and 1975 - though that in Spain came about with General Franco's death in November 1975, well over a year after the former Greek Prime Minister Constantine Karamanlis had been summoned back from his self-imposed exile in Paris, which in turn was three months after the revolution in Portugal.[225] In the broad sweep of history, however, these did come hard on the heels of each other. There may have appeared to be some parallels between the three transitions, all of which were peaceful despite having each country's army at the heart of them, but these were essentially coincidental. As Kohler puts it, "... the transition from dictatorship to democracy evolved under very specific conditions and took a different course in each country".[226]

Although there were many differences, there were also some noticeable similarities. France and Greece had been members of the United Nations since it was founded in 1945, whereas West Germany had been admitted only the year before in 1973. Portugal had taken its seat in 1955 along with several countries from the Eastern bloc such as Bulgaria, Hungary and Romania, others clearly part of Western Europe (such as Austria, Finland, Ireland and Italy) and some whose alignment was not wholly clear (notably Albania and Spain). With respect to NATO, France and Portugal had been among the twelve founding members in 1949, with both Greece and Turkey joining three years later and West Germany in 1955.[227] France was withdrawn from the military part of the alliance by de Gaulle in 1966 and Greece temporarily between 1974 and 1980 in protest at Turkey's invasion of Cyprus.

As President of France Giscard's term to 1981 was similar to Schmidt's as Chancellor of West Germany to 1982, and between them they promoted the world economic summits that started as G6 meetings in 1975 (the other countries being Italy, Japan, the UK and the US).[228] Karamanlis was Prime Minister of Greece from his return in 1974 until he became President in 1980, while Mario Soares was Prime Minister of Portugal from 1976 to 1978 and again in the 1980s. He was President for ten years from 1986.

Greece

Although he denied it, Constantine Karamanlis and his New Democracy party had a particularly evocative electoral slogan in 1974: 'Either Karamanlis or Tanks!'[229] This would have resonated with all Greeks given the military junta that had been in power since 1967, but had the added advantage that it underlined Karamanlis' democratic credentials. It was as a democrat that he thought of himself first and foremost. For example, reflecting on his first period as Prime Minister from 1956 to 1963 he would comment that "this does not mean that in my time the state of Greece was idyllic, but it shows that there was a serious and honest effort to develop the country in a democratic framework".[230] This could mean though that he thought any opposition anti-democratic:

> ... the King believed that democracy would be in danger (though not from Karamanlis) if ERE [the National Radical Union party Karamanlis led in 1963] won a fourth consecutive election; and Karamanlis believed it would be in danger if he were defeated.[231]

He went further, prophesying that "a victory for his opponents would be followed soon afterwards by a dictatorship; 'but it will not be myself who imposes it'".[232] In part this was the hyperbole of electioneering, but it should not be forgotten that the 1963 election was less than twenty years after the Nazi, Italian and Bulgarian occupation of Greece during the Second World War and the brutal civil war that followed it.[233] In addition, Greece was bordered by Communist neighbours to the north and east (Albania, Bulgaria and Yugoslavia) and the narrow Aegean Sea separated it from the perennial foe Turkey. To that extent Karamanlis may have been justified in invoking the memory and threat of subjugation.

In the event Karamanlis' shroud-waving of democracy's defeat and the threat of dictatorship failed to rouse people in sufficient numbers to vote for him and, from a majority position in 1961 with 176 seats in a parliament of 300, his party ERE was narrowly defeated in 1963 by George Papandreou's Centre Union. Voting was compulsory in Greece and with slightly more votes the Centre Union had 138 seats (up 56) to ERE's 132 (down 44). In Karamanlis' view King Paul should have limited Papandreou's mandate since he did not have enough seats to form a majority government without the support of the Union of the Democratic Left (EDA), many of whom were Communists, but the King did not and Karamanlis chose to leave the country for exile instead. In a letter to his party colleagues Karamanlis explained his decision by asserting that

> current conditions prevented him from pursuing his vision for Greece. His efforts to enact basic institutional changes had failed,

and now the political tides were running against him. His hopes for Greece frustrated, he had decided to exit the political arena.[234]

Papandreou resigned in July 1965 when he was prevented by the new King Constantine, whose father Paul had died the year before, from becoming Minister of Defence as well as Prime Minister. The King particularly objected to the move at that point because Papandreou's son Andreas was under investigation as leader of a group within the army that were allegedly seeking to overthrow the King and take over the country. Papandreou did not expect the King to accept his resignation and, even if he did, that Parliament would be dissolved and a new election called. However, the King confounded him on both counts and at the third attempt in September formed a new government known as the 'apostates' without Papandreou.[235] This government struggled on until December 1966 when the King appointed a caretaker government with a mandate to conduct elections by May 1967.[236]

Fearing that the Centre Union would win a landslide, and being unable to persuade Papandreou to postpone the election, the King and some of the generals planned a coup. But before they could act they were beaten to it in April 1967 by a group of more junior officers led by Colonel George Papadopoulos, the army's liaison officer with the CIA.[237] The Colonels, as they were known, justified their coup "by declaring that it is necessary to stop a communist threat and to cure the society of the cancer that threatens to destroy its Hellenic values".[238] Though, as Kohler points out, rather than preventing the Communists from seizing power the coup was about maintaining the dominant role of the military and preventing Papandreou's centre party from taking over government.[239]

When the King attempted a counter-coup in December 1967, a "charade" and a "pantomime" according to Silverman,[240] the Colonels ended their "pretence of rule through civilian puppets," the King fled into exile and a regency was set up with Colonel Papadopoulos as Prime Minister and much else.[241] There was little internal opposition in the early years, in part because the status quo was preserved and the economy developed strongly. However, it was a repressive regime that had shown its hand early by imprisoning thousands of Communists when it first took over, dissuading others from opposing it. Nor was there much international condemnation, for the regime

> was propped up by support from the United States, concerned more about [Greece's] vehement anti-communism than its appalling human rights record [i.e., approval of the former outweighed any disapproval of the latter]. Nor was there any united opposition to the regime by the Western European democracies. While the Netherlands and the Scandinavian countries were forthright in their hostility, Britain and West Germany voiced criticism of the regime's brutal practices but tacitly backed a country seen as vital to NATO interests.[242]

Things started to change in 1973, first when inflation shot up to double figures and then in May when a mutiny in the navy demanding the junta's resignation was exposed.[243] The junta tried to implicate the King and Karamanlis in the plot and on 1st June announced the abolition of the monarchy and

> the introduction of a republican constitution with Papadopoulos as President. There was to be a plebiscite on the new constitution ... within two months and elections by the end of 1974 [sic].[244]

According to their constitution, the Prime Minister was not to be responsible to Parliament but, as had been the historic position in Ethiopia, to the head of state, in this case the President. There were large-scale student demonstrations at Athens Polytechnic in November after Papadopoulos (the only candidate) had been elected President for the next eight years, with tanks sent to crush the demonstration.[245] More than twenty students were killed.[246] This brutal suppression and the institution of martial law escalated the situation markedly and Karamanlis' return was sought by some as the only way to reconcile the people and the military. Karamanlis chose to remain silent, no doubt judging that events spoke for themselves, but another group, this time of Generals, acted fast, thereby avenging their sidelining by the Colonels in 1967 when they had been too slow. An isolated Papadopoulos and his Prime Minister were overthrown by the chief of the military police, Brigadier Ioannidis, the power behind the coup, with Lieutenant-General Gizikis as the new President.

Ioannidis was behind the ousting of Archbishop Makarios the following May, forcing him out of Cyprus, but when Turkey responded by invading Greek military commanders refused to carry out Ioannidis' orders to attack and elements in the army demanded a return to civilian government.[247] Kohler explains that the opposition within the army, particularly that of General Davos in Macedonia, "caused President Gizikis to call a conference of leading military figures, together with a number of well-known former politicians".[248] According to Woodhouse,

> Gizikis summoned a Council of past Prime Ministers [still in Greece] and other civilian leaders ... At one point in their five-hour meeting Ioannidis was summoned and informed of the Council's intention to appoint a civilian government. Unabashed by the disasters he had caused, Ioannidis told them that they were making a mistake, but he would not resist. He then left the room in a temper. But the Council still found it difficult to agree on the composition of the new government.[249]

Various people were suggested as Prime Minister but were discarded for one reason or another, including Karamanlis who was opposed by some of the Council. Finally, a compromise appeared to have been reached but Gizikis was persuaded that no solution would be possible unless Karamanlis was part of it. Karamanlis was advised of the position but it was only when "the Chiefs of Staff came on the telephone, begging him to return at once" that he agreed.[250] He flew back from Paris to Athens the same evening on the French President's plane that Giscard had made available to him.

Karamanlis was sworn in as Prime Minister at 4am the following morning 24th July 1974. In a report headlined 'Mr Karamanlis, Greek hero or the grave digger of democracy?',[251] the *Times* described it as "a spectacular comeback" but did not underestimate the problems he faced: dealing with the Cyprus conflict; handling the diehards in the military while balancing the need for retribution with a gradual re-shaping so as not to spark a backlash and another coup (a "policy of cautious normalisation" as it came to be called); drawing up a new constitution; deciding whether to reinstate the monarchy; holding democratic elections when the political parties either did not exist or had been emasculated during the junta years.

All had been achieved by the end of 1974.

As Kohler puts it, Karamanlis relied "on those politicians from the pre-military dictatorship party establishment who had not discredited themselves by their attitude to the junta".[252] Greece was withdrawn from the military part of NATO in protest at Turkey's invasion of Cyprus, but an armed response was eschewed and the partition tacitly accepted. The constitution of 1952 was restored, political prisoners freed and the Communist Party, outlawed since 1947, legalised.[253] Karamanlis' New Democracy won a majority in the November elections, 54% of the vote translating into 220 out of 300 seats, the "amplifier effect" of the Greek electoral system delivering the stable majority Karamanlis had sought. A referendum in December 1974 rejected the restoration of the monarchy with a 70:30 split in favour of a republic. Karamanlis had remained neutral though it is argued that, had he been supportive of the monarchy's return, the result would have gone the other way. Perhaps this reflected his conflict with the monarchy in 1963 that had spurred him into exile in the first place.

A new constitution came into force in June 1975, emphasising human rights and permitting a peacetime president to temporarily delay parliamentary legislation but no longer to stifle it. Even this restriction could be overturned by a parliamentary majority.[254] Karamanlis took the opportunity of the CSCE conference in Helsinki, which Helmut Schmidt later described in his Stimson lectures at Yale University as the peak of cooperation on international security, to bring the Balkan states together in pursuit of multilateralism. As often in politics, the timing was critical because key Balkan Communist leaders were looking for "further emancipation from Soviet tutelage (Romania) or [had been] reassured that regional co-operation did not threaten their relations with Moscow (Bulgaria)".[255] In Helsinki, Karamanlis secured the agreement of Romania, Bulgaria and Yugoslavia to an inter-Balkan meeting which, when it began in early 1976, involved all the Balkan states (other than Albania) and included Turkey. Greece was feeling the loss of US protection and, whereas superpower rivalry had sometimes brought Greece and Turkey together in opposition to their Communist neighbours, the CSCE atmosphere built on superpower détente to reduce their fears over the spread of Communism. Regrettably, this also sharpened their focus on their conflict with each other.

Karamanlis called the next Greek elections a year early in 1977 to seek a fresh mandate to pursue EEC entry and to do so faster than previously planned as he expected Greece to be safer in the EEC than out. However, no longer seen as the country's saviour, its buttress between dictatorship and democracy, and judged on achievements rather than potential, the vote for Karamanlis and his New Democracy party decreased to 42%, though still sufficient to give him a majority in Parliament with 172 of the 300 seats.[256] Three years later he became President and New Democracy's electoral success ended in 1981 when the election was won by PASOK, making Andreas Papandreou Prime Minister.

France

The second ballot in the 1974 presidential election in which Giscard d'Estaing narrowly defeated Francois Mitterand (50.8% to 49.2%) to win office followed hard on the heels of the Portuguese revolution. The former on 19th May was less than a month after the MFA (Movimento das Forças Armadas) took over in Portugal on 25th April, while in between Willy Brandt had resigned as West German Chancellor on 8th May and been replaced by his Finance Minister Helmut Schmidt on the 16th. Karamanlis' return from Paris to a saviour's welcome in Athens took place two months later.

Mitterand of the 'United Left' had won the first ballot by some margin against three candidates on the right, of whom Giscard was the most moderate and leader of the Independent Republicans, the junior partner in the Right Coalition (including the Gaullists and the conservatives). In the run-off, however, the Right coalesced around Giscard as their surviving candidate and his slogan of 'Change Without Risk', differentiating him from the Socialist Mitterand who was certainly advocating change but in a way, d'Estaing argued, that threatened an "overthrow of the established order".[257] But if d'Estaing was critical of Mitterand's state socialism, Mitterand was equally dismissive of d'Estaing's patrician background that made him emblematic of the establishment. These characterisations were borne out by the results of the second ballot which saw Giscard more popular with women, those aged 65+, farmers and professionals, while Mitterand fared better among men, under 35s and manual workers.[258]

Apart from this ideological battleground, the other main one - as in most elections - was the economy. There were both historical and current dimensions to this in that Giscard had been Finance Minister from 1962 to 1966, until de Gaulle dismissed him for being an advocate of "a free-market approach to economic affairs and [seeking] a more 'European' and 'Atlanticist' foreign policy",[259] both preferences that put him at odds with de Gaulle's stance. Three years later Giscard returned to the same post under Pompidou, holding it for the next five years until Pompidou's death. With the western economy undergoing a downturn with the oil price doubling from $5.11 in October 1973 to $10.84 that December,[260] d'Estaing was perceived as vulnerable. However, the overall quadrupling of oil prices since the Arab-Israeli war was affecting many oil-importing nations across the world and had come soon after the Bretton Woods agreement had been abandoned. Neither could be laid at Giscard d'Estaing's door even if the French "stock market had lost 50 per cent of its value, unemployment was rising and inflation was running at nearly 14 per cent, three times the level of the 1960s".[261] Besides which, OECD figures show a substantial annual increase in France's GDP per head in 1974 and a smaller downturn in 1975. OECD statistics for percentage growth year on year reinforce this picture: +4.3% in 1974, -1.0% in 1975 and +4.4% in 1976.[262]

This rather reinforces Kershaw's assertion that

> ... France [like West Germany], navigated the economic storm-waves with fewer traumas than did either Britain or Italy. They faced similar economic problems as energy prices soared. But [France and West Germany] handled them better. They benefited from strong economies that could cushion the worst of the oil shock. Their governments were also under highly competent new management.[263]

Most voters would be unaware of the macro-economic picture of course, let alone those elements that would mark recovery in the future, but they would be familiar with inflation and unemployment, the micro-economic effects that had a direct impact on their pocket. And while the close result does indicate that

Mitterand had some success in blaming Giscard for the downturn, d'Estaing had countered by pointing out that Mitterand had himself been a Minister several times in the pre-de Gaulle, pre-Fifth Republic era. By drawing attention to this, Giscard was suggesting that "a man of the Fourth Republic was incapable of dealing with a modern economy".[264]

As President, Giscard d'Estaing set out to forge a "consensual form of presidential leadership", notably including the political left in the consultative Economic and Social Council that advised on parliamentary Bills and debated the traditional French five year plans. Initially the new President provided a breath of fresh air, pursuing broad policy objectives rather than adopting the interventionist approach of the Pompidou years, with his centrist position enabling him to promote modest social reforms, particularly where civil liberties and justice were concerned. Examples in 1974/75 were liberalising abortion and divorce laws, both of which were popular as well as overdue, but as time went on Giscard d'Estaing found the 'hands-off' approach increasingly difficult to sustain, "ending up significantly extending the 'presidential sector'".[265]

The French state's mix of fierce independence with an arrogant belief that the world should be following its lead is shared by many other nations (not least the USA), but is apparent as more than a stereotype in many French leaders from de Gaulle to Macron. It is better concealed, or at least moderated, at some times than others and in Giscard had a particular flavour that can be seen most clearly in his foreign policy aspirations. He continued to affirm France's independent statehood through the development and retention of the separate nuclear force that had enabled de Gaulle to withdraw France from the protection of the NATO umbrella in 1966. Giscard pursued détente with the Soviet Union and an active role in Africa and the Middle East that went beyond the country's colonial history. He sought a place for France alongside the leading industrial countries (Japan, US and West Germany) by adopting what his economists judged the critical components of the FRG's fiscal strategy (monetary control, a stable currency, balanced budget and controlled wage moderation). Indeed, France's June 1974 budget was deflationary in order to tackle rampant inflation and the surge in unemployment.

To meet his leadership ambitions and raise France's international profile he was instrumental in initiating "new institutions of European and world economic summits".[266] That this was done in conjunction with Helmut Schmidt, a long-standing friend from their days as Finance Ministers, illustrates Giscard's recognition of the political realities if France's aspirations were not to founder.

Jacques Chirac, from the Gaullist majority in the Right Coalition, had been Giscard's first Prime Minister, but in August 1976 Chirac resigned over a capital gains tax Bill, though this may have been cover for Chirac's ambitions that necessitated a distinctive platform detached from the President. And, in any case, the Gaullists were already furious over the direct elections to the EEC Parliament that had been agreed at the start of the year.[267] The impact was to make Giscard d'Estaing, the junior partner in the Right Coalition, increasingly isolated and, without a majority in the National Assembly, progressively neutered, unable to get his reforms through.[268] He replaced Chirac with Raymond Barre, whose austerity plan focussed on inflation while unemployment continued to rise, making them both unpopular. (By contrast Austria at this period always judged full employment the top priority.) Derbyshire takes the view that by the end of the 1970s, Giscard's defeat by Mitterand in the next presidential election was almost certain for he had "become an increasingly aloof and despondent figure, subject to damaging gossip and court scandals" (e.g., the diamonds that he was alleged to have received from Jean-Bédel Bokassa, the self-styled Emperor of the Central African Republic).[269]

West Germany

West Germany was fast-becoming an economic and industrial model by 1974, but this meant that it aroused envy and resentment as well as respect. Parkes underlines the significance of the ideological and value-driven difference between the free market approach (of Great Britain and the US, for example) and the social market approach of West Germany:

The role of the state in the German model [is] at least two-fold: first, to regulate the market so that optimum conditions for competition and individual enterprise were maintained and not thwarted by the growth of monopolies and cartels; and second, to ensure a social welfare system for those who might have fallen by the wayside in a totally free market system. Soziale Marktwirtschaft can thus be seen as an attempt to balance different interests, to create a climate of co-operation rather than confrontation.

This aspect of co-operation is underlined by other features of the economic order: partnership or co-determination in industry and the role of the trade unions.[270]

He also differentiates the two countries that Germany was then divided into:

> In the GDR [East Germany], it was largely impossible to sink; it was equally impossible for the overwhelming majority to rise, whatever their talents, beyond a modest level of comfort within the frontiers of one small state. There was no 'GDR dream' which could compensate for society's shortcomings. ... All too frequently it proved impossible to square the circle: to have, for instance, full employment and productive work, cheap rents and adequate housing.[271]

Whereas in the social market economy of West Germany by contrast, "The unusual or 'magic' element has been to achieve positive results simultaneously in ... four areas" (inflation, growth, unemployment and balance of payments).[272] This has not as yet proved possible in a free market economy such as Great Britain where state intervention is at a minimum and has been deliberately reduced since 1980.

There were other differences with some of Germany's neighbours too, including France.

In addition to Brandt's external initiatives, particularly his rapprochement with the East through Ostpolitik, fundamental to understanding Brandt's performance as Chancellor between 1969 and 1974 are the government's concerns about internal security, which arose from the youth protests of the late 1960s and early 1970s, sometimes developing into the terrorism that became characteristic of this period. This happened across the world, but West Germany was a particular hot-spot with the Red Army Faction (Baader-Meinhof group) one of the most feared. It was in this context that the anti-radical decree of January 1972 was introduced, preventing the employment of members of radical organisations by the German State. In practice, however, there were three problems: firstly, the German civil service is very far-reaching, extending to railway and postal employees, whose radicalism was of no identifiable risk; secondly, some of the organisations specified, such as the German Communist Party for example, were completely legal; and thirdly, the legislation was applied unevenly, with conservative States (i.e., those governed by the CDU) implementing it most harshly.[273] Brandt later admitted the decree to have been an error[274] but it had already cost him his friendship with Mitterand, who was then seeking an alliance with the French Communists ahead of his bid for the presidency and he "disparaged [Brandt's] half-hearted social democratism".[275]

Subsequently, a Palestinian terrorist group took Israeli athletes hostage at the 1972 Munich Olympics, killing eleven of them when an attempted rescue went badly wrong.

Ostpolitik directly, and the anti-radical decree indirectly, led to the bizarre situation of Brandt calling a vote of no confidence in his own government. The success and pace of *Ostpolitik* had resulted in some disgruntled members of Brandt's SPD/FDP coalition crossing the floor of the Bundestag in 1972, depriving the government of its majority.[276] Brandt then won a vote of no confidence in April 1972 called by the opposition CDU leader Rainer Barzel, who failed by two votes to secure the 249 he needed to topple the government. However, Barzel's move was widely interpreted in the country as opportunist and inappropriate, and an upsurge of support encouraged Brandt to invoke a vote of no confidence himself in order that he might call an early election that November in order to recover his majority.[277]

The election was a resounding triumph, resulting in 230 seats in the Bundestag for Brandt's SPD party, 41 for his FDP coalition partners and only 225 for the opposition CDU/CSU - though there proved to be a sting in the tail. The CDU/CSU had a majority in the upper house comprising the State governments (the Bundesrat), and the Bundesrat could put a brake on Brandt's legislation if it chose. Together with an epidemic of wage claims, a growing number of strikes and a more assertive SPD left-wing who interpreted the election result as giving them licence to promote their own agenda, Brandt's government came under pressure again.

In 1973/74 Willy Brandt and Francois Mitterand improved relations between their respective political parties, but they deteriorated again when Brandt's replacement as German Chancellor Helmut Schmidt preferred Giscard d'Estaing over Mitterand in the 1974 presidential campaign.[278] Both Brandt and Schmidt had come to national prominence through State government (Land), a not untypical route in West Germany then and Germany now.[279] Schmidt had been in the national parliament (Bundestag) previously, but it was his performance in Hamburg that raised his profile, while Brandt was Mayor of West Berlin from 1957 to 1966, defusing tensions when the Berlin Wall was built in 1961 not least by preventing crowds storming the Brandenburg Gate. He added to his national profile when he accompanied John F Kennedy on his visit in 1963, notable for Kennedy's 'Ich bin ein Berliner' speech that boosted confidence at the height of the Cold War and contrasted sharply with de Gaulle's refusal to go to Berlin in 1962 while the Wall stood.[280]

The exposure of Gunter Guillaume on Brandt's staff as an East German spy was the reason Brandt gave for his resignation in May 1974, and Brezhnev, with whom Brandt often worked closely, is supposed to have told Brandt's adviser on *Ostpolitik* that he would never forgive Honecker for letting "Guillaume carry on his mission after the Treaty of Moscow and the re-establishment of trust". In 1985, however, Honecker told Brandt that "he had not been aware of any of it at the time".[281] There were in any case several other reasons why Brandt might have chosen this moment to depart from the front-line of German politics. These are supposed to have included mounting dissatisfaction with him within the SPD party, though if there was any substance to this it is difficult to see how Brandt could have remained party leader for the next thirteen years to 1987 (five years after Schmidt ceased to be Chancellor). Perhaps of more significance was that Brandt was a visionary for whom the daily grind had begun to pall once the momentum had gone from *Ostpolitik* after the 1972 election.[282] Schmidt was much better suited to the pragmatic managerialism that was then required, as Kershaw concludes:

West Germany - and Europe - [were] fortunate to have Helmut Schmidt ... at the helm during the deeply troubled years of the 1970s. ... in dealing with the impact of both the oil shocks [including 1979] and with the growing international tension at the end of the 1970s, Schmidt's expertise and judgement [were] invaluable - and not just to his own country.[283]

However, this should not be taken to imply that Brandt's contribution was in any way less significant; only that different strengths were better suited to the challenges of different times. Illustrative of this is the comparison Schmidt's biographer draws: Schmidt's "support in the country was broader than his backing in the party, while Brandt's position was the opposite."[284] Or, as Kristina Spohr puts it, while the judgement of history favours Adenauer, Brandt and Kohl as the most significant Chancellors, Schmidt was faced with four international crises that he handled adroitly: collapse of the Bretton Woods monetary system; explosion of oil prices; worldwide recession; and the ensuing malaise of inflation and stagnation ("stagflation").[285]

When Schmidt ceased to be Chancellor in 1982, he was in effect isolated and became an elder statesman. Brandt was not only SPD leader to 1987 but President of the Socialist International from 1976 to 1982[286] and chaired the Brandt Commission from 1977, producing two reports 'North-South' in 1980 and 'Common Crisis' in 1983.[287] The UN had set individual countries a target of 0.7% of GDP as aid by 1979; the Brandt Commission increased it to 1% by 1985.[288]

Brandt had already forged a powerful coalition in the Socialist International in the early 1970s with his friends and fellow heads of government Olof Palme of Sweden and Bruno Kreisky of Austria. Furthermore, Brandt was "primarily responsible for aiding Socialist parties in Spain and Portugal ... [to] strengthen [them] against the threat of competing Communist parties" after long periods of Fascist rule.[289]

Portugal

According to Kenneth Maxwell in 'The Making of Portuguese Democracy', the CIA station chief in London claimed "When the revolution occurred in Portugal the US was out to lunch; we were completely surprised".[290] But then they did have a few other things on their mind by April 1974, including the impending Senate hearings on Watergate.

Portugal had been particularly hard hit by the oil price rise and embargo of 1973, compounded by the wars with its African colonies, so that its GDP per head declined slightly in 1974 and substantially in 1975.[291] It was already one of the poorest OECD members and it was becoming poorer. This was made worse by the 1974 revolution and the events that followed it, with some blaming the return of capitalism[292] and the exploitation of workers they thought as inevitable as night follows day, while others pointed the finger at the Marxist Communism that held sway in Portugal in the months after the revolution. What is not in dispute though is that on the eve of the revolution, Portugal

> had a very backward, unproductive agricultural system and an industrial sector that, despite rapid growth rates, failed to provide employment for a growing population because of a mistaken emphasis on capital-intensive development.[293]

Young people were emigrating, not just as they had before in order to find work, but now to avoid war as well. To great inequalities in income and wealth was added growing dissatisfaction among both technocrats and in the armed forces.

The 'carnation revolution' in Portugal in April 1974 was the bloodless overthrow of the Caetano regime engineered by the disenchanted and radicalised leaders of the MFA. As Pimlott puts it,

> ... a long period of right-wing authoritarian stagnation had given way to an explosion of Marxian revolutionary enthusiasm which, as it turned out, was to be Europe's last.[294]

Morrison agrees with Newitt that the first leader the MFA installed, General Spinola, was at the conservative end of the spectrum and whereas he judged that the change of government was enough, the radicals in the MFA (who held the upper hand then) thought this should just be the first change of many.[295] Not surprisingly, given this preference, the Communist Party were closely associated with what was now the Revolutionary Council,[296] the Communists of Alvaro Cunhal being its staunchest ally. For his part Mario Soares supported the MFA leadership to avoid the risk of what had happened in Chile the previous September, in other words of reactionary forces mounting a counter-coup in Portugal.[297] On the other hand, while he agreed that Portugal needed reconstructing "along socialist lines", he did not think this should be led by either the Communists or the military (MFA).[298] Maxwell quotes an American senator as remarking that

> There is nothing else now going on in the world - not in South East Asia, not even in the Middle East, that is half so important and ominous as the communist drive for power in Portugal.[299]

Spinola attempted a conservative take-over in September, but this was quickly closed off (by the Communists as well as by the internal security forces) and with the left now in the ascendancy General Costa Gomes was installed as the new President.

Elections were held exactly a year after the Revolution on 25th April 1975. Silverman refers to the "headline of [a] famous *Times* report" on the day of those elections as 'Capitalism is dead in Portugal', reflecting the widely expected result.[300] In fact the headline was 'Will the military be able to hang on to power in Lisbon?' and the phrase Silverman claims as the headline was a single sentence in the body of the text.[301] The overall sentiment was similar but there was no need for Silverman to have fabricated the headline (or perhaps copied it uncritically from another book). In the event, however, it was Mario Soares' Socialists who had the largest share of the vote (38%), with two conservative parties sharing 26% and the Communists only the third largest party with 18%. This conferred a legitimacy on the Socialist Party that it had not enjoyed previously and precipitated a split in the MFA between its moderate and radical wings. Over 70% of the electorate had voted for democratic parties, a result that was interpreted as their clear rejection of yet another dictatorship being foisted upon them. They had just got rid of the previous regime after fifty years and they now expected to be consulted on, and help shape, the country's future themselves.

The confusion continued and by July Soares had resigned as Foreign Minister and the MFA set up a three-man triumvirate which quickly collapsed. Matters came to a head in November 1975 when the military split, the Communist Party prompted labour strikes and the Prime Minister was taken hostage by construction workers demanding a 45% increase in wages. The military commander was replaced and another left-wing coup began. Soares continued to stand up for parliamentary democracy, now with the support of moderates in the military, notably the Army Chief of Staff General Eanes. There was a showdown on the 25th November outside the presidential palace, with the military ultimately persuaded to go back to their barracks rather than fight their own people.

> Army reforms were swiftly put in place and the power of the military was curbed. The radical left lost influence in the military. Communism was meanwhile forced to the political fringes.[302]

The army was reduced in size by three-quarters from its pre-April 1974 peak of 250,000 and its "professionalism restored".[303]

Elections took place the following February and a new Constitution was agreed from April 1976. [304] Soares became Prime Minister in July 1976, while Eanes had been elected President the previous month with 62% of the vote. He now had

> the backing of all parties except the Communists, who from now on were excluded from power. Eanes provided the necessary symbol of national unity. Soares ... was the key political player ....[305]

for his Socialist Party had 107 of the 263 seats in the Assembly.

A year earlier, on the day after the CSCE Helsinki conference, a gathering of

> socialist heads of government was held in Stockholm[306] ... The main item on the agenda was how to protect the Social Democratic movement in Portugal ... from being suppressed by either fascism or communism. It was agreed unanimously that the European socialist parties would pursue a variety of methods, including military assistance, to ensure that this did not happen.[307]

Schmidt and the West German SDP were supportive financially, but Callaghan was even more so - though this put him at odds with

Kissinger who felt that Portuguese democracy was past saving, according to Callaghan's biographer Kenneth Morgan:

> Kissinger and the American government were distinctly wary of Callaghan's policy of giving moral and other aid to Soares and the Portuguese Social Democrats. They were almost inclined to believe it might be objectively better to let the country go Communist and prevent the contagion from spreading thereafter. Callaghan believed that Portugal could be saved for democracy and indeed it was vital that it was, given its strategic position in western Europe. Events were to suggest that Callaghan's appreciation was the shrewder of the two.[308]

8.   AUSTRIA: STRADDLING ALL DIVIDES?

It is a geographical truism that Austria is at the heart of the European continent, with Vienna 1294 miles from Dublin, the most westerly capital, and 1450 miles from Tbilisi, the capital of Georgia and one of the most easterly. It is even more central on the north-south axis, 840 miles from Oslo, less than 900 from Helsinki[309] and 800 miles from Athens, the most southerly. Indeed, one map boasts that 30 different countries are within 500 miles of the Austrian capital. Even more notably, though, there is a sense in which Vienna is also at the centre of the world. Not according to Mercator's projection of course, for it is neither on the equator nor the Greenwich meridian, but in more meaningful political, social and cultural terms.

In 1945 Austria might have ended up in the Eastern bloc as did its neighbours Hungary and Czechoslovakia. Like those countries, Austria would suffer hugely in the post-war period, having endured seven years of Nazi exploitation and depredation since the 1938 Anschluss, as well as the recent devastation in 1944 and 1945 itself as the Allies fought their way towards Germany, but little more than thirty years later it was considered "more successful than the US and most other industrialised states in mastering the economic crisis of the 1970s" for, with low inflation and low unemployment, Austria "had one of the highest economic growth rates in the industrialised West".[310] How did this happen?

And how did it happen in a small country that had none of the industrial history, scale or other advantages of its neighbour West Germany that experienced a similar post-war rebirth? There were of course marked similarities between Austria and FRG, for example, in relation to their pursuit of a social, rather than free, market economy and in their determination to adopt a consensual and cooperative approach, but there were also some notable differences. Even in West Germany there was "a respectful recognition of Austria's impressive economic achievement" by May 1973.[311]

Firstly, Austria was perhaps fortunate that not only did it lie to the south of Germany, but that its own neighbours to the further south and west were the determinedly independent and later non-aligned Yugoslavia, neutral Switzerland and a battered Italy. Yet

Vienna was partitioned amongst all four Allied occupying powers, under the same quadripartite control as that adopted in Berlin, but with access to the Danube almost entirely in the Soviet sector, and with Vienna, again like Berlin, surrounded by the Soviet zone of occupation over, in this instance, about one-third of the country.

Secondly, at least as significant as the country's strong labour history and absence of a dominant middle class, was nationalisation after World War II of virtually all the assets seized by the Nazis in 1938. Then, when the USSR withdrew from the country in 1955, the Soviet Union "relinquished its grip on hundreds of Austrian enterprises" that it had previously controlled during the occupation.[312] They were taken over by the Austrian state as stakeholder and by 1963 the two tranches of nationalisation accounted for 24% of industrial output and 27% of total exports.[313] As Katzenstein puts it,

> nationalisation of a large proportion of the means of production was not so much an expression of the class struggle in a capitalist society as an assertion of Austria's national independence in the conflict among nations.[314]

As in West Germany the initial political control was inherently conservative but, probably more importantly, the government could, and in Austria's case did, comprise a coalition forged through proportional representation rather than outright majority rule by one party. The post-war coalition in Austria, known as the Great Coalition, lasted from 1945 to 1966. This fostered, or at least reflected, the country's preference for a partnership approach[315] which could neither promote nor adopt an extreme stance, nor have governments that veered from one extreme to the other, if it was to remain representative and retain the support of the wider electorate. Like West Germany and other European countries such as the Netherlands and Sweden, but unlike those with first past the post democracies (notably the western free market exemplars the US and the UK), Austria "opted for systems of proportional representation rather than majority rule, thus showing an early willingness to share power among disparate political actors".[316] This is a statement about values and beliefs, and ultimately about the country's culture of equality at the forefront of

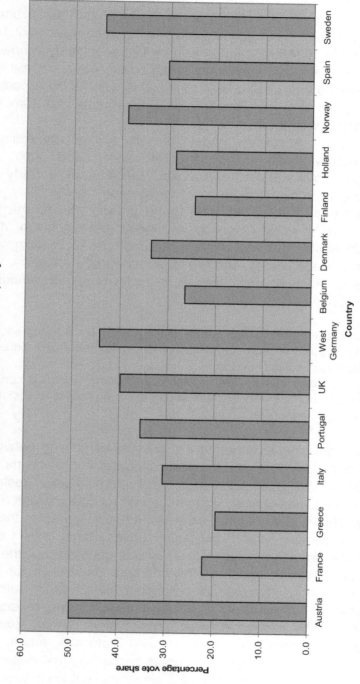

Figure 1: Average vote share for main Left party in fourteen European countries from 1970-1979
from Sassoon, pp461-468 and Table 2 above p63

its commitments. Universal suffrage might be a *sine qua non* for the demonstration of liberty, but if the views of half the country are ignored, where is the equality and what chance fraternity? The UK since the 2016 referendum on Europe is a case study in how not to do representative democracy, with over 48% of the voters marginalised and treated as if their views were of no account. It is only a small step from this inflexible, dismissive and authoritarian approach to dictatorship.

Also, Austria's model of shared accountability and responsibility extended to the civil service and public sector company boards with the Socialist (SPÖ)/People's Party (ÖVP) balance even in boards of management of publicly owned undertakings.[318] It is but a minor leap from this to the default position, as in West Germany, of worker representation at board level. In Austria this was achieved through the close links with few and large trade unions, and the other economic and labour interest groups to which all employees were legally required to belong. For Katzenstein,

> Austria's democratic socialism is distinguished by a strong socialist party, a powerful and centralised union movement [and] extremely centralised political institutions …
> In a capitalist society that it helped transform, Austria's Left has moved from the theory of class struggle to the practice of social and economic partnership.[319]

There is a continuous process of political bargaining between the interest groups, State and the political parties in order to maintain a consensus. For example, Katzenstein refers to wage restraint by the trade unions being explicitly traded off for concessions on social policy. This is not unique, and was perhaps less so in the 1970s under social democratic and labour governments than it is today when unionisation in many countries has declined, but the upshot for Austria was to underline the country's preference for equality over efficiency, whereas its neighbour Switzerland, with which Katzenstein compares it, is widely known for the reverse.[320] In addition to the obsessive Swiss pursuit of efficiency, anonymous and secretive companies dwarf a rump State, whereas in Austria, which voluntarily engaged in informal bargaining that depended on trust and mutually agreed social aims, the outcome was always open to public scrutiny and debate, and consequently to amendment and adjustment.

By the 1980s Austria, and Vienna in particular, was thought of as being at the crossroads, not only geographically, but of the north-south and east-west ideological divisions and differences as well: **of** both camps, but **in** neither. When it is not described as the 'island of the blessed', it is thought of, for example, as a bridge between the US and USSR superpowers and between the wealthier north and the more impoverished south (globally as well as in Europe). OPEC moved their headquarters to Vienna in 1965, the United Nations opened their UNO City there in 1979 and the Organisation for Security and Co-operation in Europe (OSCE, the permanent successor to the 1974/75 CSCE) is not alone among international organisations in choosing to base itself there.[321] The country's capital has hosted negotiations with the PLO, diplomacy discussions more generally[322] and strategic arms limitation talks (SALT I and SALT II).[323]

Switzerland's long-standing neutrality made Bern, Geneva and Lausanne attractive locations for international organisations, but in May 1955 Austria guaranteed its future neutrality in a treaty with the four occupying powers.[324] This came into effect that October, enabling the occupation to wind down. Seven years later Austria joined the European Free Trade Area (EFTA), two years after Portugal, and subsequently following it into informal membership of the EEC in 1972. It took Portugal until 1986 to become a full (rather than associate) EEC member and Austria almost another decade to 1995, expanding the EEC to fifteen countries as Finland and Sweden joined at the same time. Greece had predated all of them, becoming the tenth member state in 1981.[325]

In the 1970s it was Austria's lasting neutrality and its social partnership model that, combined with its tourist profile, made it particularly attractive to outsiders - not just for organisations determined to demonstrate their ideological independence. But there were at least three other significant factors: the centrist election programme in 1970 that had seen Bruno Kreisky elevated from Foreign Minister, the post he had held from 1959 to 1966, to Chancellor; his appointment of Rudolf Kirchschläger as his Foreign Minister who, as Ambassador in Prague in 1968, had himself offered Czechoslovakian dissidents refuge in Austria, contravening the orders of his superiors in Vienna in order to do so;[326] and the importance of the individual over the State, a stark contrast, and in direct opposition to, the Soviet model of Communism as practised in the Eastern bloc, and alongside it the gradualist approach re-affirmed by Kreisky in the 1970 election that favoured reform over revolution.[327]

Making promises during an election is one thing. Delivering them once the votes have been secured is another, particularly once the Austrian economy, like all others in the west, worsened in 1975. Consequently, the social partnership model was vital in seeing the country through but so was the leadership provided by Kreisky. As Jelavich puts it, "… the government and the institutions of the social partnership were able to handle the accompanying problems …".[328] Or, as Fitzmaurice explains, the pillars of the Austrian model were active neutrality, accompanied by political and social consensualism, the latter evidenced through the Economic and Social Partnership, a parallel coalition to the political one between the two main parties. Fitzmaurice continues:

> A key component in the Austrian political system, and perhaps its most significant characteristic, is the permanent search for compromise, balance and involvement, through the broad participation and cooperation of all major political actors in the process.[329]

It was this preferred approach, in West Germany as well as Austria that was hugely significant in the EEC and then the EU arriving at the most critical decisions through unanimity. In other words, all countries had to agree in order for a substantial change to be pursued. In some instances countries sought an opt-out where they accepted much of a Treaty but not its entirety (e.g., Britain's opt-out from the Maastricht Treaty social chapter). Thus an individual country's sovereignty was never threatened. Quite aside from the ratification process by individual countries of Treaties, the prerequisite for all major decisions was unanimity.

Part of the leadership challenge was (and is) to manage expectations and nowhere is this more apparent than in the discussions between Kreisky and the head of the Trade Unions, often settling "important political questions in informal and secret bargaining sessions" between them.[330] Both the government and the Trade Unions appreciated that employment is valued more highly than price stability in Austria; and in tackling the economic crisis of the 1970s, the government adopted a counter-cyclical, Keynesian approach that sought to "counter-act market developments through massive deficit spending before giving more serious consideration to its limited options for a structural policy".[331] The approach was pragmatic and eclectic, a combination of Friedman and Keynes, that Kreisky, speaking of the overall social and economic partnership, characterised as "a marriage without love which works".[332] The Trade Unions for their part have kept strikes to a minimum (about three minutes per worker were lost on average in 1972)[333] and

> subscribe to the linking of productivity and wage rises over the course of a full business cycle and do not seek to reach their broader social and economic objectives through collective bargaining.[334]

Union wage demands did rise in 1974/75, hence a counter-cyclical stance from the Unions at that time too, with a shorter working week introduced in 1975 so that fewer jobs were shared among more employees, thus holding down the number unemployed - as was also achieved by 33,000 workers accepting early retirement and holiday entitlement increasing from three weeks to four.[335]

Kreisky has drawn attention to the parallels between Austria and West Germany, and the lessons that many other countries could learn from their consensual approach and social market model: "there were only two countries in the Western world to produce ... high levels of employment, satisfactory growth and moderate inflation."[336] Kreisky ascribes this assessment to a report to the US Congress by Professor Wassily Leontief of New York University, the specifics of which are not cited, but it is the case that in a 1979 Congress report on economic change Leontief's verbal evidence reflected on the importance of this approach to economic growth in the 1970s:

> In Austria, another country that successfully resists inflationary pressures, the institutional set-up is very similar to that ... [in West

Germany] except that the Government plays a greater role in across-the board negotiations between trade unions and employers' organizations. It does so by contributing rather detailed input-output type projections of economic outlook for some years ahead.[337]

It may not be entirely coincidental that there were similarities in their backgrounds between Brandt and Kreisky, indeed they had met each other as long ago as 1940 according to Jelavich,[338] as well as parallels in their careers. For example, both were refugees from Nazi Germany, Brandt in Norway and Kreisky in Sweden, both would be their country's Foreign Minister before becoming Chancellor and, as leading European Socialists, both would be prominent in the Socialist International (along with Olof Palme of Sweden) in later years.

In the 1974-1980 period Austria developed and expanded economic relations with the socialist economies on its doorstep, extending lines of credit (particularly to Poland where Austria was one of the major creditors), thereby building on the Austro-Hungarian tradition while maintaining good relations with the west. As an example of the latter, lacking its own car manufacturer and threatened by low cost imports from Asia, Austria attracted General Motors in the 1970s, partly by the government subsidising one-third of the start-up costs. Like the earnings from tourism, then equivalent to one-third of all Austria's exports of goods and services, this helped keep the trade deficit in check.

As the government was expected, and expected itself, to ratify policy objectives agreed between interest groups (such as the three sub-committees of the country's long-standing Joint Commission)[339] rather than determine them, the model that emerged was planning-free (Austria had given up "serious attempts at economic planning" as early as 1949),[340] a marked contrast to the ultimate planned economy of France and dependent on an intuitive and collaborative policy process to be effective. Katzenstein says the general verdict on the impact was "cautiously approving" in 1984,[341] though it was much less positive by the end of the 1980s after the Waldheim affair, problems in state industries and a series of political scandals.[342] In the 1970 election Kreisky's SPÖ party was the largest for the first time since World War II, obtaining an absolute majority the following year.[343] As long as he and his

Finance Minister were in harmony, the country worked well but once they fell out in the 1980s, with Kreisky sacking him in 1981, deficit spending increased and unemployment rose to 5% by 1983 (the highest level since 1960). Adhering to the country's model of social democracy was not enough to save Kreisky and he resigned as Chancellor rather than form a minority or coalition government after the 1983 election.

9. CENTRAL AND SOUTH AMERICA: CIVIL DISORDER AND REPRESSION
(Uruguay, Chile, Colombia, Bolivia, Guatemala)

By the early 1970s the military was in charge, from the south of the continent to the north, in Argentina, Brazil, Paraguay, Bolivia, Peru and Ecuador, and had huge influence on the civilian regimes in Colombia and Venezuela. Even in Chile, Salvador Allende's Cabinet included the heads of the armed forces from November 1972.[344] Only in four countries, three of which were on the north-east coast of South America and were not strictly part of Latin America (Guyana, Suriname and the overseas department of French Guiana), was this not so. These three countries had Commonwealth, Netherlands and French links respectively, and only in French Guiana had there been any substantial Spanish involvement in their history. The fourth country, and the one with the longest democratic tradition on the continent, was Uruguay. Uruguay was then, and is now, the smallest country in Latin America whether measured by area or population.[345] It is sandwiched between its much larger neighbours of Argentina and Brazil on the eastern coast and shares the River Plate basin with Argentina. From time to time Uruguay has acted as a buffer between these two pre-eminent powers in the region, and its story has often been over-shadowed by them.

However, these factors are not enough on their own to explain why Uruguay's history in the 1970s is so little known, while that of Chile on the western coast had an apparently similar story in the same period but the overthrow of democracy in that country in 1973, with Salvador Allende replaced by General Pinochet, is a staple of political analysis. This must have something to do with expectations and hopes, with Chile having less democratic tradition than Uruguay[346] and one that was snuffed out overnight, whereas the transformation in Uruguay was a gradual slide into authoritarianism over several years and one in which some of the civilian authorities were complicit and others stood by, ineffectual and wringing their hands. There might also have been a view that the rise of terrorism in Uruguay, the Tupamaros urban guerrillas (the Movimiento de Liberación Nacional or MLN, sometimes rendered as MLN-T), could only be ended by the military. But do the facts bear this out or was it another myth and convenient cover for the repression of the population and the removal of their rights?

Both Uruguay and Chile are covered below, though with more space given to the former than the latter precisely because events are just as arresting but comparatively unknown. Bolivia and Colombia are included for their illustration of the Latin American spectrum - as is Guatemala from Central America, for though it also received less foreign interest and attention than its El Salvador and Nicaragua neighbours, it too was representative of repression and terrorism. By contrast the other countries in the region, Belize, Costa Rica, Honduras, Mexico and Panama, were relatively peaceful during this period.

Uruguay

In his 1975 book 'Uruguay: The Politics of Failure', Martin Weinstein poses the question "How and why did a nation that was regarded as so different from its neighbours so quickly 'fall' and come to resemble them?"[347] Weinstein identifies the conflict between urban and rural ideologies that increased after the death in 1929 of the modern state's first president and founder, Jose Battle y Ordonez, who had come to power twenty five years earlier after a civil war and set the country on a democratic, socialist and interventionist path. For Weinstein,

> Battle's conception of social justice required an activist, interventionist state, for only such an over-riding institution could ensure the protection of the collective interest.

The options were either for the state to act indirectly as regulator to ensure that standards were adhered to in the interests of all, or "directly as the provider of essential services and the owner-operator of key commercial and industrial activities". Battle preferred the latter, not least because it was the most effective way of countering foreign exploitation and the danger of becoming mired in foreign debt. The crucial tests for Battle of whether monopoly or competition was more appropriate were the national need and public interest.[348] He had demonstrated the importance of the latter, and his pro-labour credentials, as early as 1905 when the first national syndicate, the Workers Federation of the Republic of Uruguay (FDRU), had been established.

Battle's preferred mechanism was co-participation, which encapsulated his democratic ideal of stable civil politics, but after his time it became warped to justify the establishment serving its own ends rather than those of the nation, "supportive of a powerful clientelistic politics" incapable of "change and reform" as Weinstein has it.[349] To this should be added the urban/rural dichotomy, which to all intents and purposes meant the ideological gap between the capital Montevideo, which remains the heart of Uruguay with over 50% of the population, and the rest of the country. Known as Battlismo after the President's death, his philosophy was rooted in the city and focussed on "the concepts of development, citizenship and social change" whereas the counter-ideology of rural interests promoted "the values of hierarchy, tradition and order". The latter, dominant from the 1940s, "ultimately circumvented the very institutions" Battle and his colleagues had created.[350]

Alongside this longer view, Weinstein and others are explicit about the immediate causes of democracy's slide since the 1960s as economic decline and the rise of the Tupamaros urban guerrillas. It was to the country's detriment that a weak president who had vacillated between the two main political parties, the Blancos and the Colorados, as best suited his fortunes, was elected in 1971. Juan Maria Bordaberry (1928-2011) was an advocate of ruralism to the extent that he had any adherence at all, and was severely undermined by being the proxy candidate of his predecessor as president Jorge Pacheco Areco (1920-1998) who had first tried, and failed, in a 1971 referendum to get the Constitution changed to allow a sitting president to put himself forward for a second term. It was then expected that Bordaberry would be his puppet, but the military exposed some dubious activities of Pacheco Areco and his lifestyle in Spain which eliminated his hold over Bordaberry.[351] Pacheco Areco had himself been unexpectedly elevated from vice-president, a post that had previously been turned down by two others, when the incumbent president Oscar Gestido died shortly after his inauguration in 1967. Neither Pacheco Areco nor his successor Bordaberry were "first rank", had little political standing or party profile beyond their own clique,[352] and Bordaberry inherited the disastrous decisions Pacheco Areco had taken in his presidential term to 1971. Bordaberry would surpass them in 1972 to 1976.

Bordaberry's obituary in the *Guardian* is forthright:

> [His] name … will be forever associated with the slow death of a democracy at the hands of those entrusted with its care. The word *bordaberrización* was coined to refer to the way this elected president first bowed to military demands for control of the executive, then became an enthusiastic advocate of military rule. So enthusiastic, in fact, that even the armed forces ultimately balked at his fascist ideas, replacing him with pliant yes-men.[353]

There had been a coup in 1933, four years after Battle's death, but this was orchestrated by a democratically elected Battlista president in response to the Great Depression of 1929 and justified on the basis of a necessary constitutional reform. Parliament had been dissolved, but President Terra's regime was a soft dictatorship that lasted nine years to 1942 and became known as the 'good coup'.[354]

However, there was nothing that could be remotely described as 'good' about the 1973 self-coup (*autogolpe*) unleashed by Bordaberry when he dissolved the National Federation of Workers (Convención Nacional de Trabajadores, CNT) and suspended parliament in June 1973.[355] This may have been initiated with a flimsy rationale about tackling terrorism, but it soon became state-sponsored terror. People without arms "faced the onslaught of the army and police massacring them" as they took to the streets in an attempt to restore democracy,[356] for the main labour confederation had called a 24-hour strike the day after the *autogolpe* but, when half a million trade unionists rejected the coup, it became a general strike. It collapsed after fifteen days and the CNT was declared illegal.[357]

Kaufman identifies three stages from October 1972, when the military confronted parliament with the support of the president, to the military coup in June 1973,[358] but the breakdown of democracy had begun long before then. There had been economic stagnation and increasing social unrest since the 1950s.[359] As Weinstein characterised it in a later book:

Mobility in Uruguay was a myth that died. Its demise would lead to increased social and political tensions that would put an end to Uruguay's exceptionalism in Latin America - the exceptionalism of a stable, middle-class democracy.[360]

An estimated 700,000 people had emigrated between the 1963 Census and the 1975 one, with a consequent loss of skilled young people, destabilising the country's welfare system and leading to a corresponding deterioration in the country's morale.[361] In 1968 President Pacheco Areco imposed a wages and price freeze and abolished the wages councils that had involved both sides of industry in negotiating wage settlements for the previous twenty-five years. The following year strikers, even private sector employees, were called up into the army and told to return to work. If they refused, they were tried as deserters. The alleged reason for this 'militarisation' of strikers was to prevent sabotage, of which there might have been some risk in the electricity generation and oil refinery sectors but not for most people employed elsewhere. This extraordinary response to strikers by the army was the first of three major errors by the politicians that inflated the military's view of its critical role in the state, a view compounded by democracy's self-inflicted implosion. The second and third substantial errors were to allow the army a free hand in the campaign against the Tupamaros in 1971 and then to follow up this abdication of political accountability by turning over part of the judicial system to them, allowing them to handle subversion trials as they saw fit from 1972.[362]

The Tupamaros' armed struggle, probably influenced by Castro's successful revolution in Cuba, had begun in the early 1960s to secure social progress and had an impact out of all proportion to the small numbers involved.[363] In the absence of widespread support in his party, Pacheco Areco demonised the Tupamaros and set himself up as the "champion of the established order against subversion", enabling him to bypass parliament and impose his chosen policies in the name of public safety.[364] This included the suspension of habeas corpus in 1971.[365] Within six months of Bordaberry's inauguration in 1972 the Tupamaros had been comprehensively defeated. This ought to have heralded a period of stability but instead became a harbinger of the disasters to come for the army were now out of control and when the civilian government sought to re-establish their authority in February 1973 they were ignored - not only by the army but also by fellow politicians who failed to rally to their support. Indeed the army forced Bordaberry to accept a National Security Council to oversee his actions.[366] As politicians began to flee the escalating repression, it became easier for the military to step into the vacuum and claim they had the solution to the country's economic problems as well - helped tacitly by those citizens who welcomed the military crackdown as the only way to "overcome internal strife".[367]

Due to the idiosyncratic operation of the presidential election system, the Uruguayan Senator Wilson Ferreira Aldunate had been defeated by Bordaberry in the 1971 election. Under the 1967 Constitution the political parties, of which the main ones were the Blancos and Colorados, could nominate more than one candidate each, with each of their candidates from different factions within each party. "The elected president will be from the faction which received the largest number of votes [within] the party that polled the [most] votes."[368] In 1971 Bordaberry received a lower number of votes than Ferreira Aldunate but the three candidates from different factions in the Colorados (one of whom was Bordaberry) polled more strongly overall than the two Blanco candidates (one of whom was Ferreira Aldunate). Bordaberry secured the most votes among the Colorado candidates and was therefore elected. The candidate of the left was Liber Seregni, standing for the coalition of left-wing groups Frente Amplio he had helped to form in 1971 after his retirement as an Army General.[369] He was imprisoned soon after the *autogolpe*. Ferreira Aldunate fled the country in fear for his life as soon as parliament was dissolved.

Ferreira Aldunate was one of the most articulate opponents of the Bordaberry dictatorship, writing the foreword to Kaufman's 1979 book, and it was he, Weinstein and Kaufman who testified before the US House of Representatives Committee on International Relations in June and July 1976 on the torture and abuse of human rights that was by then widespread in Uruguay.[370] Ferreira Aldunate asserts that Bordaberry fancied himself as a dictator but the army were beyond his control, justifying their takeover in June 1973 as "removing the breeding grounds of subversion".[371]

In September 1974, fifteen months after the military took charge, "a petition ... calling for the re-opening of parliament and the revival of civil and political liberties" was summarily rejected.

> Many of those who signed the petition had been parliamentary colleagues and political supporters of Bordaberry until the military takeover.
> Even though some political observers believe that the President may personally wish to see a gradual introduction of political freedom before his term of office comes to an end in 1976, the fact remains that the military leaders were not impressed by the petition. It was indirectly addressed to them and in turn rejected by them.[372]

With good reason, Kaufman describes Bordaberry as "a civilian stamp that legitimised the arbitrary demands of the military,"[373] but this "figurehead" role did not last long for, after a dispute in 1976, the military replaced him with an elderly lawyer Dr Aparicio Mendez. When the military took control in neighbouring Argentina in 1976, the

> dictatorships of South America's 'southern cone' [Chile, Uruguay and Argentina] set up Operation Condor, under which their secret police collaborated in capturing and 'disappearing' each other's dissidents.[374]

Eventually, but not until 2006, Bordaberry was found guilty of planning the murder of political opponents and subsequently sentenced to thirty years imprisonment for a variety of offences including repeatedly violating the Constitution. He spent the last five years of his life under house arrest because of ill-health.

At the end of the 1970s Amnesty International reported on political imprisonment in Uruguay, condemning the erosion of the rule of law, the abuse of human rights and noting that in less than a decade Uruguay had been turned from a beacon of democracy to an example of the most severe repression on the continent. As in the Latin America Bureau briefing referred to in the Introduction, Amnesty International concluded that

> Since 1971 when political imprisonment began to take place on a larger scale in Uruguay, the number of political prisoners has varied

from a few hundred to 5,000-6,000 and, according to exile sources, has even reached 8,000. In 1976, Amnesty International estimated that 1 in every 500 citizens in Uruguay was in prison for political reasons and that 1 in every 50 citizens had been through a period of imprisonment, which for many included interrogation and torture. These figures reflected the frequency of short-term detention without trial of trade union activists and the numerous arrests made during 1975/76, mainly of members or supporters of the Uruguayan Communist Party. In 1979, according to Amnesty International's records, between 2,500 and 2,800 prisoners of conscience and other political prisoners are being held in the various military and civilian prison establishments and military barracks used as places of detention. This still means that one in every 1,000 citizens is a political prisoner ...[375]

In addition more than half a million had gone into exile and more than 100 people had been "disappeared" after arrest, either in Uruguay or in neighbouring Argentina.

Yet, in a clear illustration that some consider economics more important than people, it was still possible for the London-based Overseas Development Institute to assert the same year that

Of the three monetarist stabilisation programmes adopted in Uruguay, Chile and Argentina in the mid-1970s, the Uruguayan programme was the most successful.[376]

Some might consider this an odious comparison, precisely the league table that you would not want to be in, but for those people not in prison or under the threat of it this did indicate that life had improved a little. The threshold was not high for inflation was 44% in 1978 (down from 77% in 1974) after a freeze on wages and prices in 1975, but for many unemployment was already the reality or posed a greater risk.

The ex-Army General and Frente Amplio presidential candidate in 1971, Liber Seregni, played a significant role in the post-1982 negotiations that led to a return to democracy in 1984. The military, recognising that his involvement was critical to the left-wing and their acceptance, had released him from prison about halfway through a 14 year term imposed in 1976. By contrast Ferreira Aldunate was refused permission to return from exile and was excluded from the negotiations. When he re-entered Uruguay in early 1984 without permission, he was imprisoned.[377] Neither Seregni nor Ferreira Aldunate were allowed to stand in the elections.[378]

Chile

In 1974 the population of Chile was about 10.43m people, less than four times that of Uruguay,[379] but it covered more than four times the area (292,000 against 67,600 square miles). Overall, therefore, Chile was less densely populated yet the impact of this was more apparent than real for the overwhelming majority of the population clustered around the Santiago/Valparaiso area as they do today. Nevertheless, outlying settlements would be more isolated than in the more urban and tighter Uruguay, and the elongated and mountainous Chile would certainly have more transport and communication difficulties.[380] William Davis stresses the importance of geography to South American countries - indeed this applies to all countries, even in Europe, that are geographically spread and less industrialised/urbanised than in western Europe - a factor all too easily forgotten by those accustomed to giving most weight to history.[381] This would prove particularly relevant in Chile in October 1972 when, as the US ambassador since the previous October explains, a "partial national truckers' strike began" to forestall the possibility of nationalisation by the government.

> Chilean truckers were fiercely independent-minded entrepreneurs. Most owned a single truck or, at most, two or three. ... In a country shaped like a string bean, the 47,000 trucks that carried goods up and down the land were of vital importance.[382]

This was just one of the strikes that put Allende's government under pressure at this time, "alienated ... much of Chile's middle-class" and led to the existing Cabinet standing down in order to "give the president a free hand".[383] Allende's next Cabinet from the start of November 1972 included military officers.[384] There would be several more Cabinets over the next nine months, most but not all including the military in political roles, but few lasted long as the country became more volatile.

William Davis also concludes that some people in South American countries might prefer a stable dictatorship to a corrupt and ineffective democracy. This appears to have been an element in Uruguay's decline into dictatorship for, just after the *autogolpe*, the *Wall Street Journal* asserted that

> Despite scattered opposition, it appears that most Uruguayans are resigned to the abridgement of their liberties. Many people seem to prefer stability (even on horseback) to turmoil and instability.[385]

Before accepting this at face value, however, it should be remembered the audience it was written for, one that might put economic interests before human freedoms. (The patronising reference to 'horseback' also gives an insight into this US lens.) Additionally, Uruguayan voters rejected by 57% to 43% the military's proposed constitution in November 1980 which, even if the military was no longer all-powerful, was, individually and collectively, still a courageous outcome. Linz and Stepan make the point that, as in Portugal, electoral success conferred a legitimacy on the democratic opposition that it did not have before.[386] For Weinstein it signalled the beginning of the end of the military.[387]

Needless to say, democracy may exploit some, particularly the poor and voiceless, but dictatorship (unless benevolent) exploits more, often nearly all, and may do so through a climate of fear as well as imprisonment and physical torture. Democracy in Uruguay might have proved itself ineffective in tackling the economic problems the country faced but it was not alone in this. Rather its liberalism was deeply unpopular with hardliners in the military just as the Allende government in Chile was unpopular with both internal and external forces. Weinstein makes the point that the Uruguay military sought to save the country not only from the guerrillas but even more "from the liberal Battlista legacy that had nurtured the left, grown corrupt and had ultimately proven itself incapable of overcoming Uruguay's economic crisis".[388]

Furthermore, the shift towards concentrating executive authority in the president, and away from parliamentary democracy, is apparent in Chile's history as well as that of Uruguay. The 1970 constitutional reforms, for example, made executive decrees usual and limited the role of Chile's Congress. This in turn opened the door to dictatorship and the army commander-in-chief General Pinochet burst through. The Uruguayan military by contrast had slammed it shut in the civilian Bordaberry's face. Once in power, and even though part of a four-man junta to begin with (alongside the heads of the navy, air force and police), Pinochet relied on the verities of military discipline and the Latin assumptions of tradition and hierarchy to accrue authority and become *primus inter pares*. Pinochet's aim was to destroy the Left and restructure Chile's political institutions.[389]

The military coup in Chile started in the early hours of Tuesday 11th September 1973, less than three months after the final stage of the Uruguayan slide into military rule, and Allende died the same day. Two days later the military rulers in Uruguay and Brazil recognised the Chilean military government and the US did so within a fortnight. In the intervening ten days twenty-two other countries had formally recognised the take-over including, it is claimed, European democracies such as Austria, Denmark, France and the UK.[390] If this seems unlikely, it should be noted that Austria was the only one of these countries with a socialist government, nor should diplomatic recognition necessarily be the touchstone for assessing a country's response:

> In the weeks after the coup, most European countries allowed people fleeing the junta to take refuge in their embassies in Chile. The main exceptions were Britain, Germany and Denmark, whose governments ordered their embassy staff to turn away asylum-seekers.[391]

Pinochet's brutality was swiftly denounced by socialist leaders in Europe including Palme, Kreisky, Mitterand and Craxi, and as many as 100,000 Chilean exiles found refuge in Europe.[392]

Within weeks, Chilean local government and higher education had Pinochet's appointees in place, political parties were banned or dismantled, free speech was restricted, the press censored and TV hijacked to promote the regime's vision. "Thousands were arrested, 'disappeared', or killed" as the security apparatus swung into action.[393]

If the military takeover in Uruguay suited US policy by encouraging its diversion to a "pro-American course",[394] US influence was less subtle and more blatant in the overthrow of Allende in Chile. There are several examples in the US ambassador's memoir. For example,

Nixon and Kissinger were reported to be furious at Allende's election in September 1970, with Nixon supposedly referring to "that bastard Allende" five weeks later.

In November 1970 when the State Department first suggested that Davis might be moved from Guatemala to Chile:

> At the time … I had no knowledge of covert action in Chile and little knowledge of the depth of hostility to Allende in the White House, although I realised that the US government regarded Allende's election as a sharp setback to US interests.

As James McCord told the Senate Watergate Committee, the Chilean embassy in Washington, DC had also been bugged (probably on the weekend of 13th to 15th May 1972) by the same 'plumbers' who broke into the Watergate building.[395]

Nathaniel Davis underscores the US covert role elsewhere in his book, including a long chapter with that title in which he points out that

> It is widely believed that the United States 'destabilised' the Chilean government in order to bring it down, fomented and financed demonstrations and strikes, and made common cause with right-extremist subversives.[396]

The US Senate in 1974 tasked its Select Committee on the Intelligence Services (the Church Committee) to examine the CIA's role in Chile in the previous decade in order to establish whether these were more than just 'beliefs'.[397] The Committee reported on the substance that lay behind them in 1975. Meanwhile several investigative journalists (not least Seymour Hersh in the *New York Times* and Jack Anderson in the *Washington Post*) had exposed CIA actions at the time. The US role has since received the attention of academic historians, for example Jonathan Haslam whose 2005 book on the subject includes on its cover a silhouette of Allende over the rubric "A case of assisted suicide".[398] Nixon had instructed the CIA Director on 16th September 1970 (twelve days after the Chilean elections) "to block Allende's confirmation" and "make the economy scream".[399] The CIA failed in the first but, with the assistance of the International Telephone and Telegraph Corporation (ITT) and major copper companies, contributed to the second.

In the same news conference at which he justified pardoning Nixon, President Ford claimed that CIA funds had been used "in the best interests of Chile".[400] This was despite the US State Department having confirmed the previous January that thousands had been killed during the coup.[401] Ford may have believed that CIA funds (and initiatives) had been directed towards supporting the democratic opposition to challenge the Allende government constitutionally rather than overtly to destabilise it, but at the very least this was naïve and self-serving. It would not be borne out by the evidence the Church Committee uncovered. On the day after Nixon's pardon the *Times* had carried Seymour Hersh's report of a secret hearing in which Bill Colby, then Director of the CIA, had confirmed to the Senate a "$8m operation to topple Allende" authorised by Nixon.[402] Nathaniel Davis writes of a twin-track approach that was only partly visible even to the US Ambassador.[403]

As a further illustration of the impact the coup in Chile had in Europe compared to the ignorance of the situation in Uruguay, the *Times* newspaper carried 480 reports on Chile in 1974 against a handful about Uruguay. Beef from Uruguay was nothing like as important to the west as the copper mined in Chile, and this would be a further explanation why Chile was covered more prominently: oil was not the only commodity on which western economies depended. Foreign-owned copper mines in Chile had been expropriated by Allende's government, and compensation had yet to be finalised, but the Pinochet junta confirmed to the UN that they would not be returning them.[404]

Even with the acquiescence of the middle-classes, the military junta took time to establish the stable dictatorship that William Davis posited as a South American preference. In February 1974, almost five months after the coup, the report of the respected

Chilean journalist Florencia Varas was headlined "Make or break time for the Chilean regime":

> Military tribunals dispense summary justice, armed patrols appear on streets and highways, checking identification papers, and a midnight curfew in Santiago (and at other hours in the provinces) constantly reminds Chileans that the situation is not entirely normal.[405]

The country was officially "in a state of siege" and the junta relied on the claim of an "internal state of war" to justify their continuing crackdown. Meanwhile, prices had increased by 800% since the junta took over, with wages lagging far behind this rampant inflation. Seven months later on the anniversary of the coup, little had changed (though inflation was down to 200% per year): "Still a state of war a year after Allende's fall" for, as the *Times* journalist Peter Strafford's account made clear,

> It has turned out to be a particularly authoritarian and, at times, brutal form of government, far more so than many people expected ... Even now, there is no indication of whether or when the military will relax its grip.[406]

Support among the middle classes contrasted starkly with repression and torture for the junta's opponents for there were "Two worlds under Chile's junta".[407]

Three months earlier Pinochet had become head of state and sole leader of the junta.[408] It would be another sixteen years before power was transferred back to a civilian government in 1990 and then only because Pinochet failed to receive majority support in a 1988 plebiscite for a further eight years in power to 1997.[409] But he remained head of the army through to 1998 with the "prerogative of unremovability", as the other three members of the junta also had, and all four were voting members of the eight-person National Security Council (the same descriptor as that forced by the military on Bordaberry in Uruguay). Furthermore, the incoming civilian government was required to adopt and operate under the existing authoritarian constitution that Pinochet had devised in 1980.[410] Although the new government of President Aylwin had a clear electoral mandate from 1990, it took time for this legitimacy to be translated into power. Even in 1993 to 1995 "military acts of intimidation and defiance of the democratic government" persisted.[411] Linz and Stepan draw the parallel between Mitterand's criticism of de Gaulle's Fifth Republic as a "permanent coup d'état" with the straightjacket confining the Chilean government, inherited from Pinochet and designed to insulate him when President, and from which they could escape only gradually as the economy improved.[412]

Colombia

Peru was also under military control at this time but the regime was unusual in being reformist and "progressive-minded.[413] Although it would be absurd to compare it to Allende's administration in Chile, it found itself isolated in South America once the Chilean government's approach and objectives had been dismantled by Pinochet's coup.[414]

Another extreme on the continent was represented by the "qualified democracy" of Colombia which from 1958 had been governed by a bipartisan coalition comprising the two main parties operating together as the National Front. The president alternated between the two parties until 1974 with parity in all executive, legislative and judicial posts.[415] The first competitive elections since 1946 took place in 1974 whereas prior to that the electors shaped the composition of the Congress but had no say in determining the president or the balance of the government. Indeed, in the sixteen years before 1974 the Conservatives and Liberals had two of the four presidents each, taking turns in the top post.[416] Hartlyn contends that "inclusively authoritarian" or a "managed democracy" might equally describe the result.[417]

Apart from articles on the rising price of coffee, commodity markets more generally, or success on the tennis court, Colombia received little coverage in the British press in the early 1970s. It would be different at the end of the decade when the FARC guerrillas (originally formed in 1964) confronted the government openly and the export of drugs, particularly cocaine, earned the country a notoriety and profile that had previously eluded it.[418] The presidential elections in April 1974 were reported twice in the *Times*, firstly as bringing an end to the country's "tradition of meaningless elections" and secondly four days later when the Liberal Alfonso López Michelsen won the poll by a huge margin with 55.6% of the vote.[419] His nearest challenger, the Conservative Gómez, secured 32.0%, followed by Maria Rojas of the National Popular Alliance (La Alianza Nacional Popular, ANAPO) with 9.5%. Over five million people had voted, 57.1% of the electorate and the highest participation rate for some time.[420] One tradition that the country had not given up though was elitism, for all three of the candidates came from political dynasties. The fathers of both López and Gómez had been Presidents themselves, and Maria Rojas' father had stood in the 1970 election when he had, to some minds, been defrauded of victory.[421]

López started as a reformist and, with such a substantial victory behind him, there were high hopes of his administration. But it petered out in a morass of corruption allegations and financial scandals in the country and recession across the world.[422] Although Palacios refers to the period from the 1970s on as "a crisis of legitimacy" in Colombia, the country fared better than many in the early years. There was a "flood of foreign exchange from coffee exports" so, unlike many others, there was no need to devalue and borrowing was kept under control, favouring Colombia when the second oil price shock came at the end of the decade. Less positively, the country's "hopes for export diversification [were] soon ended by world recession" and inflation continued.[423]

A clear strength of Colombia was that it avoided the mistakes of its neighbours, reflecting on their repressive and depressing experiences under military rule, not least their inability to deal with guerrilla insurgencies though this had frequently been the stated justification for abandoning civilian rule. Colombia maintained a commitment to democracy instead. There could hardly be a greater contrast with Bordaberry and Pinochet than López's response in September 1977 when, faced by strikes by all three union confederations, inflation at 33% and demands from all the top military leaders for new legislation of the "national security" type that Uruguay, Chile and others had pursued, López responded that "changes on that scale would require a constituent assembly ... but when the Supreme Court declared the idea unconstitutional, he let the matter rest".[424]

Bolivia

At just under five million people in 1974, the Bolivian population was less than a quarter of Colombia's 24 million and under half that of Chile. Bolivia covers a similar-sized area to Colombia (424,000 square miles against 440,000) but is substantially larger than Chile (292,000 square miles) and is, therefore, the least densely populated of the three by some margin. All three countries were on a different scale to the densely packed population in Uruguay and were much less developed compared to its standards of literacy, general education and political emancipation as well. Bolivia was not exceptional for the peasant, subsistence lives that many of its people led, nor for the extremes of poverty and wealth that were true in every country on the continent, but Paraguay is the only other South American country that is landlocked. Furthermore, and unlike Paraguay, Bolivia did once have a small coastline but had lost it in the nineteenth century War of the Pacific, failed to negotiate suitable terms with Pinochet for access to it in 1977 and, not having included Peru in the discussions, was unlikely to secure its return. Indeed, Peru's objections to its omission sealed their opposition to any settlement that Bolivia and Chile might have reached.[425]

Between Ché Guevara's death in Bolivia in 1967 when he failed to foment an uprising that would, he hoped, provoke the US to launch a Vietnam-style response and a collective reaction in consequence from *all* of South America, and the seizure of power by General Hugo Banzer in 1971, there had been two reformist military regimes in the country: General Ovando's from 1969-1970 and that of General Torres in 1970-1971. Both sought to promote workers' rights and improve civil liberties, the former based on the Peruvian military's 'revolution from above' and the latter a home-grown populist movement which included, briefly, a Popular Assembly or workers' council. It was ended by the conservative Banzer who modelled his rule on the repression of the military regime in Brazil.[426] Indeed, the derivative nature of Bolivian politics can be traced back to the influence of Trotsky as well as Castro's Cuba.

The Popular Assembly (set up under Torres) of 220 delegates comprised a mix of working-class organisations (60%), middle class and peasant groups (30%), and political parties (10%).

It met ten times in the ten days between 23rd June and 2nd July 1971 before adjourning to 7th September. One of the Assembly's first decisions had been to respond to any coup attempt by "a general strike and the immediate occupation of workplaces", a matter they planned to discuss further when they re-convened. However, they never got the opportunity for, with the encouragement of Brazil and Argentina, Banzer took control before they could meet again, launching a coup on 19th August. According to Sándor John, 100,000 ordinary Bolivian people demanded on the following day (20th August) that Torres provide them with arms so that they could resist Banzer's takeover, but Torres refused in order to avoid a bloodbath, a decision that was selfless as well as courageous. The miners who did fight were massacred.[427]

Dunkerley explains that the Banzer dictatorship survived for seven years because of support from the expanding bourgeoisie around Santa Cruz, particularly private mines, assistance from Brazil and through military and other aid from the US. Dunkerley asserts that the latter reflected Nixon's assessment that, "in view of Banzer's 'great courage', 'we want to do everything possible to help you'". The Bolivian economy was opened up to foreign investors while the labour force was kept impoverished.[428] For Vanden & Prevost, Banzer's "policies protected the newly prosperous middle-class and economic elite ... [but] repressed labour, peasants, students and most political parties".[429]

Between 1973 and 1974 oil profits tripled, strengthening Banzer's economic and political authority, as did the nearby examples of military regimes in Uruguay and Chile. And as in Uruguay, Bolivia's 'Obligatory Civil Service Decree' meant anyone could be forced to take state employment and therefore "be subject to military discipline", restricting workers' rights further. In 1974 Banzer mounted his own *autogolpe* ("self-coup") and established his rule as a "personalist dictatorship", postponing 1974 elections and banning political and trade union activity in the wake of an attempted coup by junior officers. [430]

From 1977, however, Banzer's grip weakened. The failure to recover the country's coastline from Chile was part of the reason, but even more significant were economic decline with oil profits reducing, growing foreign debt and punitive interest rates on short-term loans. Popular discontent grew and became more open, as did international opposition to a particularly barmy scheme, 'racism in reverse', to settle 150,000 white immigrants from Namibia, Rhodesia and South Africa on land around Santa Cruz. Fortunately, this plan was abandoned during 1977 when "an advance party of Rhodesian farmers decided … [there was in]sufficient infrastructure to sustain profitable enterprises".[431] The crunch factor, however, was the new Carter administration in the US that not only championed democracy and human rights but favoured constitutional and democratically elected governments. With the portents clear by November 1977, Banzer announced elections for 1978 and in the following January first an unrestricted amnesty for political prisoners and then removal of all restrictions on Trade Union activity.[432]

Despite his ignominious departure as dictator, Hugo Banzer would be elected president nearly twenty years later, serving from 1997 to 2001,[433] the latest in a succession of short-lived, corrupt and/or fraudulently-elected presidents who oversaw the country before the first indigenous President Evo Morales began his remarkable fourteen year term in 2006.[434]

Guatemala

In 1974 Guatemala was in the midst of "nearly four decades [1954-1991] of sporadic civil war",[435] in which about 200,000 civilians died or were 'disappeared'. In what by now may be a familiar refrain about events in this part of the world, Reilly continues "[this] left the military strong, consistently well-financed, often over-riding the executive branch of government" and in his words there had been a "decimation of rural leadership and organisation". The latter may sound like Uruguay, but similar circumstances prevailed in Ethiopia and other African countries. The immediate cause for the start of the Guatemalan conflict, the overthrow of then president Arbenz, was his land reform programme that angered the US, raising their fears that Guatemala might prove "a beachhead for Soviet expansion". The overthrow of Arbenz was undertaken through a CIA covert operation that subsequently provided the template for Cuba in 1961 and Chile in 1973.[436]

The procession of presidents, many of them generals, that had characterised Guatemala during the 1950s and 1960s continued into the 1970s. At the start of the decade General Carlos Arana Osorio was elected president. His obituary in the *Independent* newspaper described him as the "first of a series of ruthless military presidents of Guatemala". The only quibble might be whether he was indeed the first, but he was certainly not the last. He stayed in office until the next election in 1974 when he was replaced by General Kjell Laugerud Garcia,[437] who like many, if not all, of his predecessors had come to power on the back of electoral fraud He survived until the 1978 election, when the same electoral sleaze and malpractice took place and a different general took over.

In 1972 guerrillas known as the 'Guerrilla Army of the Poor' (EGP - Ejército Guerrillero de los Pobres) had entered Guatemala,[438] their activities uncoordinated and sporadic, but only brought to a halt for a time by the massive earthquake that shook the country in February 1976. There was a surge of popular and trade union unity but, as is often the way after such cataclysmic events, the gains did not last, let alone translate into social progress, and the enthusiasm of the population soon waned.

Despite this 'internal conflict' as it was known to Guatemalans themselves, Guatemala City also played its part on the international diplomatic stage and had hosted the 1971 conference to amend the Warsaw Convention of 1929. This is a somewhat surprising link to the first paragraph of this book on the Paris air crash in March 1974 for the Guatemalan Convention (as the outcome of the conference was called) raised the compensation to be paid to victims of air crashes from $7000 to $120,000. Jerry Wiggin, Conservative MP for Weston-super-Mare, asked in the House of Commons about this on 14th March 1974[439] for the Guatemalan Convention had to be ratified by thirty countries for it to be added as a protocol to the Warsaw Convention (with the added proviso that five of these countries had to account for 40% of air traffic in 1970).[440] This had still to happen then and Wiggin also wrote to the *Times* newspaper about the implications for the bereaved families of this gap in international law.[441]

10.   LIBERAL RESURGENCE: CANADA AND AUSTRALIA

Pierre Trudeau (1919-2000) and Gough Whitlam (1916-2014) became leaders of their political parties, the Liberal Party in Canada and the Labour Party in Australia respectively, at much the same time but they were different personalities who emerged in very different circumstances.

Trudeau was minister of justice in Lester Pearson's Liberal Cabinet when, in April 1968, almost five years to the day after he became Prime Minister, an exhausted Pearson announced his resignation. The Liberal Party chose Trudeau to succeed him and one of his first acts as the new Prime Minister was to call an election for June 1968. Not only was Trudeau "untried", as Robert Bothwell describes him, but he was virtually unknown to the electorate.[442] In politics for only three years, having been an academic lawyer previously, he was both a novelty and an enigma, unmarried though nearly fifty and having attended universities in four countries.[443] On the face of it, therefore, his background ought to appeal to both the English- and French-speaking constituencies in Canada, but his unconventional style and relaxed demeanour, as well as his refusal to countenance Quebec separation, made many voters wary. Might he prove to be too much a man of the 1960s when Canada, still willingly attached to the British monarchy but seeking to keep up with its north American neighbour at the same time, would prefer someone who reflected the traditional views with which they felt more comfortable? Bothwell adds:

> Trudeau's place on the ideological spectrum was also a mystery. He was a liberal before he was a Liberal, but he was realistic enough to be willing to make the compromises that party leadership demanded.[444]

His speeches emphasised the 'Just Society' that was of its time and might be expected to draw the younger vote in particular, even though Trudeau was more than twenty years older than many of them (almost thirty for some). But this was the television age and Trudeau's sound-bite politics and open, candid approach fitted the medium. He was younger than many of his opponents of course and, while this might have made him appear callow and inexperienced, his sentiments and values were in tune with those of the age and carried him through.

In Australia, meanwhile, Gough Whitlam had been a politician for fourteen years when he became Labour Party leader in 1967, having wrested the party from his predecessor Arthur Calwell and set it on a new course. Yet the dapper Whitlam, three years older than Trudeau and a political operator to his fingertips, might have passed for a conservative - which in Australian terms meant he could have joined either the Liberal or National parties, both of which vied to be the more conservative depending on the issue. His values and determination to tackle inequalities wherever they lay put him on the same track as Trudeau, but further down it, and with more certainty about how to deliver change. His self-belief was well-suited to a country that had never doubted itself - for if Australia was confident of anything, it was its own lifestyle, attitudes and future. Canada, on the other hand, had still to emerge from under the sheltering wing that Britain and America provided and demonstrate that it had an identity separate from both. There could never be any doubt of Australia's sense of itself, individual and individualistic, whereas Canada could be characterised by the collective and co-operative struggles that had helped forge it. The histories of both countries were still significant to their present orientation but meant that they had developed very differently. The native populations had been overtaken by white settlers in both cases, but only in Canada had there been other struggles that defined the country's position in the world (between the French and British, and then, largely symbolically, between Britain and the US). Not for Canada the splendid isolation that enabled Australia to evolve independently at its own pace.

Internal separatism might be part of Canada's story but it was Australia's exceptionalism internationally and 'mateship' that were far better known.

Canada

Canada's GDP grew through the 1960s, though from a very low base, until 1974 and then, after a brief interruption, continued through to the start of the 1980s. Yet for Bothwell, it was "discontent as much as affluence" that was the crucial determinant of the country's path.[445]

Shortly after his re-election for a second term as USA President, Nixon ordered that Haiphong and Hanoi be bombed over Christmas 1972. The Canadians protested formally, including in parliament where Trudeau was now the leader of a coalition government having lost his 1968 majority in the 1972 election.[446] This was just one way in which his coalition partners the socialist New Democratic party were making their influence apparent.[447] Nixon was furious, but what the USA considered Canada's effrontery in making its views known so publicly was soon forgotten as an international peace-keeping force might be necessary to cover the withdrawal of US troops and Canada's commitment to this would be vital. In the event the Watergate scandal engulfed every other US objective and disabled whatever their strategic intentions might have been (see Chapter 5 above).

In May 1974 Trudeau's government was defeated in a vote of confidence on its proposed budget when the New Democratic party, worried that they were becoming too closely identified with the Liberals after eighteen months of sharing power, voted with the opposition Progressive Conservatives. It was worldwide inflation that had brought the government down for, while there was no dispute that Canada was powerless to alter the international economic situation, there was disagreement over how the government could and should mitigate its effects domestically. The Liberal response was judged inadequate by 137 votes to 124 and a defeated Trudeau called a general election for July.[448]

Whereas the relaxed campaign Trudeau had run as a newcomer in 1968 had put him in tune with the country's *zeitgeist*, his 1972 campaign had gone too far in this direction. He had spectacularly miscalculated. At the start of the 1974 campaign, Trudeau was asked about his approach this time. The journalist had

prefaced his question by sardonically describing Mr Trudeau's disastrous last campaign, or non-campaign, as 'a work of art'.
The Prime Minister replied that he was grateful for that description and added dryly that one takes consolation where one can. He went on to say that he intends to fight a vigorous campaign, but not a violent one, 'to see as many Canadians as possible for as long as possible and to put the issues squarely before them'.

To take him at his word, voters can therefore expect to see a different Mr Trudeau in action from the one whose leisurely progress through the country in the fall of 1972, whispering sweet nothings in their ears about how strong the land was, led his party within a whisker of defeat at the polls.

… His incredible 'dialogue with Canadians' was exactly the wrong formula to use on a nation troubled by unemployment, inflation and other pressing problems.[449]

Nor had Trudeau's obvious loss of temper in public and his resort to expletives helped.

Although the pundits predicted another minority government in 1974, Trudeau "emerged triumphant", recapturing the majority he had lost in 1972:

[He had] forsaken the carefree antics of 1968 to adopt a more hard-hitting style of campaigning. He has used his quick mind and sharp tongue primarily to pour scorn on his opponents.[450]

The *Times* had become a fan again, with a leading article the following day applauding Trudeau's win: "He has been a better Prime Minister in the past eighteen months under pressure than he was when he first carried his party to victory".[451]

Nor were the pressures confined to the political and diplomatic, for now a married man the nervous disposition and ill-health of his wife Margaret were widely documented in the press that summer. She was hospitalised for almost a fortnight in September and then collapsed in October when accompanying her husband on a visit to France and the EEC in October.[452] The purpose of the trip was to hold discussions with the French President and Prime Minister (Giscard d'Estaing and Chirac) in Paris, and with EEC leaders and the NATO Secretary-General in Brussels. Trudeau was hoping to forge a close link with the EEC to further reduce Canada's dependence on trade with the US. There was expected to be a year's delay in reaching agreement, but it eventually took until 2014 to develop the ambitious trade agreement that had become Canada's goal by then as well as the European Union's (as it had since become).[453]

Australia

In an echo of Jose Battle's approach to developing the State in Uruguay and making it fit for purpose for the twentieth century, Gough Whitlam argued early in his career as Labour leader after 1967 that

> the capacity to exercise citizenship ... was determined not by an individual's income, 'but the availability and accessibility of the services which the community alone can provide and ensure'.[454]

This quick-stepped Australian politics from the "shibboleths" of the unionised man (and in Australia they were mainly men in the 1950s and 1960s), and the pursuit of higher wages and better conditions which had obsessed his Labour Party predecessor Arthur Calwell, to a socialism that encompassed equity and access, a society fair for all, even the Aboriginal indigenous people. This might be a commonplace elsewhere but in Australia it would be revelatory. And Whitlam soon capitalised on these modernised expectations with energy and skill, demonstrating that he planned to deliver on his promises. With the Australian facility for a memorable phrase, it might be known as the difference between 'lip and grip'.

Yet, as in Canada, an election was forced in Australia in mid-1974 and again the issue was money. Trudeau's government had been defeated by the defection of its coalition partners over its handling of inflation; Whitlam's Labour government would be denied the necessary financial resources, technically 'supply', that any government requires to fund its services and activities and so keep going. In the case of Whitlam's Labour government, it was the Liberal opposition who forced the issue. A leading article in the *Times* on 11th April explained that, while Whitlam had won a majority of nine seats in the House of Representatives at the 1972 election, Labour was just in the minority in the Senate and the Liberals were using this margin to frustrate some of Whitlam's plans to transform Australian society and had now refused the supply that the government needed to function.

Having rejected a call for an election only a few days earlier, Whitlam now resorted to a double dissolution of both houses of parliament, the first such since 1961.[455] In theory, Labour had an ideal election slogan: 'The Aristos of the Senate are frustrating the will of the people'. But would Australia still be dazzled by the whirlwind with which Whitlam had come into office in 1972, implementing the programme promised in that election "at a gallop,"[456] or had a reaction set in? As the *Times* put it,

> For all its free-wheeling, levelling style, Australia is at heart conservative. It wants change, but not too fast. Its cool distrust of politicians leads it to support the dispersal of power between states and the federal centre. It is wary of the motives behind left-wing centralism. And for the moment the bread and butter issues do not help Mr Whitlam, as inflation accelerates and strikes proliferate.[457]

Whitlam had recent vivid experience of the federal/state controversy when, a couple of weeks earlier, he had been punched and kicked when visiting a Perth rally in the Western Australia state election.[458]

Whitlam had influential support, including from Patrick White, the Nobel Prize-winning novelist, and from the Assistant Secretary in the Aboriginal Affairs Department, himself an Aborigine, who believed history would judge Whitlam the best Australian Prime Minister ever. Unfortunately, the latter had also antagonised the parliamentary opposition by calling them a rabble,[459] and it was not clear, even with the equal pay for women legislation introduced by the Labour government, that there would be sufficient support for Whitlam to renew his mandate. Opinion polls two weeks before the election on 18th May forecast a narrow defeat for Whitlam despite the charisma bypass of the Liberal leader Billy Snedden.

As well as the lengthy electoral lists confronting voters for each of the Senate and House of Representatives contests, the ballot papers included four constitutional referendum questions and it was estimated that voters could require fifteen minutes to complete what was more complicated than a "crossword".[460] It took a while to count all the votes, almost a month for all the seats in the Senate, but by the end of May it was clear that Whitlam and Labour had won a very narrow victory, a reduced majority of five seats in the House and level-pegging in the Senate.[461] All four referendum questions were voted down. In conceding the election, Snedden was clear that the close result meant that Whitlam had no mandate to transform Australia, let alone "socialise" it.[462]

It would be early August before the new Labour government finally got its disputed legislation through parliament. Stymied by the absence of a majority in the Senate, the government had invoked the constitutional provision that enabled a joint sitting of both houses to break the logjam in such circumstances. Even then Queensland threatened a judicial review of one aspect of the legislation (for a petroleum and minerals authority) and that regarding a health scheme would require further enabling legislation before it could come into operation in 1975.[463] The Whitlam whirlwind of 1972 had been reduced to a gentle breeze.

The Labour Party budget in September reflected the agenda of change and equality that Whitlam espoused, but it provided further grist to his sternest critics in the states, often the Premiers and particularly Jon Bjelke-Petersen of Queensland, for it did little to tackle inflation, the major issue facing the country, and reinforced their abhorrence of federal over-reach. The Labour Party went down to a crushing and humiliating defeat in the Queensland state election that autumn and like many beleaguered leaders Whitlam looked to bolster his position abroad in the hope that this would also translate into greater popularity at home. His discussions in Europe on improved trade mirrored those of Trudeau and Canada, and might have had the result Whitlam desired except that the failure to tackle inflation was soon compounded by the even more visible spectre of increasing unemployment.

There had been floods in Brisbane at the start of the year that ravaged 850 square miles and left more than 8000 people homeless.[464] On Christmas Day Darwin was 'crushed like a matchbox' by a cyclone. Neither natural disaster led to huge loss of life, but the remaining population of Darwin had to move elsewhere while it would be much of the year before the residents flooded out of their Brisbane homes could return.

But, if 1974 had proved politically, economically and physically destructive, 1975 was to be even worse. Malcolm Fraser took over as Liberal party leader in March 1975, the Whitlam government was once again denied the necessary supply, and after months of stasis the British governor-general Sir John Kerr dismissed Whitlam in November and installed Fraser as caretaker Prime Minister instead.[465] Whether Kerr had exceeded his powers was soon an academic question, for the Labour Party were trounced in the ensuing election in December. Eighteen months after they had voted for the new agenda Whitlam promoted, and the changes he had wrought since 1972, Australians reverted to their conservative comfort zone. The promised transformation of Australian society had been rejected; the socialist whirlwind not just quelled but snuffed out - at least for the time being. The trade union leader and future Prime Minister Bob Hawke reckoned the increasing unemployment reflected a deliberate strategy, a way of holding down the wage increases that inflation would otherwise lead to. Perhaps because the Whitlam years were subsequently viewed more positively than they were at the time, the man himself has become one of the country's most revered.

11. UNDER THE GROUND: OIL AND OPEC/MIDDLE EAST MUSCLE

What was unusual was not that producers should flex their muscles. Rubber producers had attempted it in the 1930s as car and tyre manufacture recovered after the 1929 crash and the global depression that followed. As the Irish novelist JG Farrell put it,

> ... the official policy of the Restriction Committee was not to make a killing out of rubber but merely to ensure ... 'a reasonable return to an efficient producer'. ... [but] the Committee's idea of what represented 'a reasonable return' began to rise ...[466]

What was extraordinary about the OPEC price rises in 1973 was the ideological motivation that underpinned them. The aim was not to make a profit but to strangle western support for Israel or at least make their economies squeal. Substantial oil-producing countries were not confined to the Middle East, and nor were members of OPEC (Venezuela, for example), but it was the Arab producers in the Middle East who exerted the most influence on oil production and on OPEC, particularly Saudi Arabia. Often the current (or a previous) Saudi Arabian oil minister was Secretary-General of OPEC, as was the case with Harvard-educated Sheikh Yamani, who was Saudi Arabia's Minister of Petroleum and Mineral Resources from 1962 to 1986 and in the OPEC post for twenty-five years from shortly after its founding in 1960, when there were but five members. OPEC subsequently moved its headquarters from Geneva to Vienna in 1965 and became an increasingly visible organisation on the world stage.

However, the genesis of what would become OPEC can be traced back to 1928 when three oil conglomerates dominated. They are still with us today. As an article in the *Atlantic* magazine explained in 1983:

> The international oil cartel traces back to a grouse shoot at Achnacarry Castle, in Inverness, Scotland, in September of 1928, which was attended by the heads of the three most powerful oil combines in the world: Sir Henri Deterding, the chairman of Royal Dutch Shell; Walter Teagle, of Standard Oil of New Jersey (now Exxon); and Sir John Cadman, chairman of Anglo-Persian Oil (now

BP).[467] Under the pretext of engaging in sport, these three men conspired to eliminate competition in developing new oil resources for the world [for] ... all agreed to divide future markets among themselves according to the shares of the market they held in 1928. This meant that there would be no advantage in 'destructive competition' ... among themselves for new oil fields; whatever advantage one company received would be shared proportionally by the others. In a separate 'pooling' accord, the three companies also agreed to share their oil tankers, refineries, pipelines, and marketing facilities with each other. As the membership of the cartel expanded to include the other major companies, it became known as the Seven Sisters. The cartel controlled oil production, refining, transportation, and sales in almost all areas of the world except the United States ...[468]

The example that OPEC adopted can be clearly discerned but with the key difference that it was no longer the West that controlled oil production and distribution. The 1950s had sparked the growth of national autonomy and self-government as empires were dismantled and countries decolonised, and the same process had been applied by states that expected to profit from their mineral wealth themselves and to end exploitation. The West, the 'imperial masters', had often paid only nominal, and sometimes no, royalties for extraction rights. Iran, for example, nationalised its oil wealth in 1951, though Anglo-Persian (now BP) would still get it out of the ground under licence on their behalf. The situation worsened in the 1960s when the US, previously self-sufficient in oil, became a net importer. It might be surmised that fighting wars overseas, particularly Vietnam, partly accounted for this, but the critical aspect was that once the oil advantage of the west was destabilised in this way, prices began to rise. Although 1973/74 was some years after many of the consequent changes in self-determination had worked their way through, it would not be surprising if it still rankled with more authoritarian elements in the USA and Europe. When OPEC then ratcheted up the pressure by exercising the muscle that their own oil resources gave them, in support of the Egyptian and Syrian offensive against Israel, many of these authorities would have been apoplectic: bad enough that the mineral wealth had been (rightfully) repatriated, but now it was they who felt they were being disadvantaged.

The OPEC action was far from unanimous according to the article in *Atlantic*:

> Another price explosion followed the announcement by Saudi Arabia and other Arab states, in October 1973, that they were cutting back on their oil production and embargoing shipments of oil to the United States and other supporters of Israel. [Yet] many OPEC states (including Iran, Indonesia, Venezuela, Ecuador, and Gabon) actually increased production (and even a few Arab states in OPEC, notably Iraq and Algeria, did not reduce their production). It was almost exclusively an initiative of Saudi Arabia, which was backed vocally, if not materially, by its Arab allies.[469]

In addition, Saudi Arabia secured an oil embargo, implemented through OPEC against Portugal, the Netherlands and South Africa as well. It was

> lifted on Europe (though not the USA) by November 1973 after the European Community had issued a statement interpreted as being relatively favourable towards the Arab position in the Middle Eastern conflict.[470]

The remaining embargo on the US was lifted in March 1974.[471] Venezuela had shipped oil to the US throughout the boycott, a prime factor in the start of GDP growth in that country (though, as this was its single product, the country's economy would be sensitive to any adverse effects, such as US demand reducing or tariffs increasing).[472] Despite this Venezuelan bail-out, US inflation increased. According to Maier, sustained inflation came from the "combined results of American deficits, ending [the] Bretton Woods system, labour pressure on wages [and] OPEC price increases".[473]

The Ninth World Energy Conference in September 1974 in Detroit, Michigan was opened by President Ford and the irony of the conference taking place in the 'gas-guzzling' car capital of the western world did not escape him. He stressed, as he had at the United Nations the previous week, that

> The attempt by any country to use one commodity for political purposes will inevitably tempt other countries to use their commodities for their own purposes.[474]

The Americans had responded to the oil embargo by establishing 'Project Independence' and Ford now called for 'Project Interdependence' to bolster a co-operative international approach. The first steps towards this had been taken, also the previous week, by the twelve nations that formed the Energy Coordinating Group of the Washington Energy Conference. The intention was to deal with emergencies such as the embargo, and reduce the likelihood of future ones, by

> sharing available oil and by cutting consumption and using stocks on an equitable basis. While seeking conservation, we and the other nations will work for expanded production of both conventional and nonconventional fuels. The cooperating countries are also creating an international agency to carry out this program.[475]

The western economies were understandably in earnest but the impact in the twentieth century was limited. Kershaw adds that, true to form and its determination to maintain its independence, France would have nothing to do with the International Energy Authority (IEA) subsequently established by the USA and fifteen other countries in November 1974, judging

> that participation might harm its own relations with OPEC, while Britain and Norway, which had discovered their own off-shore oilfields, reserved their right to take independent action.

There are few products that do not depend on oil, in their manufacture if not in their raw ingredients, as well as in the energy to produce them. The impact of increased oil prices was to inflate prices and to stagnate growth. In combination, an outcome that classic Keynesian economics does not anticipate, the effect on many economies was stagflation (inflation **and** stagnation) and rising unemployment as companies became uncompetitive or sought to maintain their profitability by increasing productivity (output per person) or squeezing wage rises and decreasing costs that would have otherwise enabled employees to manage the inflation that had become a routine feature of their lives.

It is more than a commonplace, almost a reflex, for observers to describe the oil price rises as leading to global recession. This was certainly the case for western economies that were heavily dependent on oil but lacked their own resources and particularly if they were both net importers of oil and a strong backer of Israel in the Yom Kippur War. This was notably the case for the UK and the US, as well as for some smaller economies in the west that were unable, or unwilling, to find alternative supplies that might have prejudiced continuing support from the US and risked the protective cocoon in which the alliance had wrapped them. But it was far from true for all - even among OECD economies (see footnote 4). Robert Skidelsky has explained the complexity faced by individual countries in a recent book.[476] Denis Healey, UK Chancellor of the Exchequer at the time, reflects in his memoir on the errors and mistakes that countries made: many governments cut their spending to reduce imports and thus "produced an unnecessary recession"; others such as Italy and Britain had already received support from the IMF and kept their spending up in line with their commitments to the IMF.

> This was a mistake, since my first budget made Britain's balance of payments worse; we exported less than we expected because world trade was shrinking [stagnation]. It is not possible for a country like Britain to grow alone when the rest of the world is contracting.[477]

The situation was made even worse by the Treasury grossly under-estimating the borrowing required (Public Sector Borrowing Requirement, PSBR) and grossly over-estimating company liquidity. By autumn 1974 inflation was 17%. Healey relied on various initiatives to bring it down (e.g., the social contract agreed between the trade unions and the government to hold down wages), but the outcome instead was vastly increasing unemployment through the rest of the 1970s. Combining the evocative image of the lengthening dole queue with a government under pressure, 'Labour Isn't Working' was the landmark general election poster that propelled the Conservatives into power in 1979.

The response of the Australian government was similar: "In 1975 it tackled inflation with a contractionary budget, and unemployment passed 250,000. The golden age was over."[478] Britain with its larger population would have been delighted with a dole queue of that size but in Australia it was catastrophic - especially as few women then worked outside the home and this meant in effect that one quarter of a million families were in straitened circumstances. The Prime Minister of Australia Gough Whitlam had been dismissed in November 1975, but his motto "crash through or crash" would echo hauntingly in the ears of his successor.

Oil was not the only commodity on which the West depended, though those that were produced in many countries, copper for example, were less likely to have artificial shortages generated as bargaining chips against the West. The political allegiances of such countries were likely to vary widely and, even if they attempted a united front, it was probable that some could be bought off. Yet one of the lessons from the OPEC action nevertheless was that western economies might be vulnerable more generally:

> The action of a number of oil exporters in limiting supplies, embargoing shipments, and driving up prices has raised the question of the extent to which consuming countries are exposed to the effects of similar collusion among exporters of other critical materials. The recent tight supply situation for energy, food and many raw materials has also prompted a more general concern— that we may be passing from an era of abundant supplies into one of constant shortages.[479]

The US was judged most vulnerable in relation to bauxite, platinum and chromium among nineteen non-fuel materials examined in this 1974 National Security study. Jamaica was the main supplier of bauxite then (though other producing countries would soon join them) with the Soviet Union the primary producer of platinum and chromium. The main internal options to sustain adequate supplies were to establish a national strategic stockpile or give end-user companies tax breaks for holding their own supplies. International arrangements were also considered in order to secure supply, including extending exporter obligations through the General Agreement on Tariffs and Trade (GATT), and multilateral discussions through the OECD. Needless to say, the pursuit of détente remained of fundamental importance for this reason too. In addition, monitoring risks to supply and prices became a routine part of government responsibility and oversight in order to forestall future difficulties.

12.   LESSONS FOR THE FUTURE: A WORLD IN FLUX NOW

The key lesson from the OPEC dispute could have been of inter-dependence between countries and of an inter-dependence that was about more than trade. The 1974 National Security Study referred to on the previous page might have been extended to the impact across the world of non-economic, as well as economic, actions that failed to be sensitive to local requirements and circumstances. This would have been enlightened but incompatible with an 'America First' approach. We are often told today of the need for all countries to observe the rules-based system that the UN fosters and represents, and warned against those countries that go 'off piste', allegedly acting counter to these rules. What this often means, however, is that they are behaving in accord with values that do not contravene the international system but do jeopardise the interests of the West. The two are not the same. Sometimes it simply demonstrates that other countries now have as much muscle as the US did in 1974 and are displaying it.

It might be assumed that the world would have advanced significantly in the fifty years since 1974 and in some ways, particularly technologically, it has. But it is as striking how little progress has been made in many areas vital to human existence[480] and how in others change has taken a gradual, evolutionary form. Among the latter, for example, agendas relating to women, and equalities and liberties generally, are being replayed.

We are more aware today that the media giants have annual revenues that exceed the gross domestic product of many countries and hold information that increases their power and influence exponentially, but the same issues were being raised about their telecommunications predecessors in the 1970s. President Allende of Chile had a special reason for being wary of the US company ITT, but in a speech to the United Nations in December 1972 he made the following points:

> The power of [all these multinational] corporations is so great that it transcends all borders ... We are facing a ... collision between the great ... corporations and sovereign states ... [But the corporations] do not have to answer to anyone and are not accountable to ... any parliament.[481]

These issues remain at least as critical today.

Even in the 1970s sovereign states, including the superpowers, did not have it all their own way. Apart from the catastrophic experiences of the US internally and externally, the USSR was wracked by dissension that would bring about its demise within fifteen years. The Cold War was economically as well as liberally unsustainable. China remained wrapped in its own difficulties, more of an enigma to observers than an actor on the world stage. Within fifteen years of 1974, the Yalta compromise would be over. The US had lost its way, the USSR was losing its and China had yet to find one outside its boundaries. Compromise though both Yalta and the Helsinki CSCE (Final Act) might be, even perhaps because they were, they demonstrated that there was a greater goal beyond individual interest. They stood out from the majority of diplomacy that was predicated on the 'one of us' principle, that is to say, each country was 'either with us or agin us' and 'my enemy's enemy is my friend'. The shorthand was 'communism versus capitalism', sheltering sometimes under the preferred rubric of 'communism versus democracy', though as has already been pointed out the US preference was for other countries to follow their ethos and conceal, or at least minimise, their own national interests accordingly (analogous to the 'might is right' power of the playground bully). It would not be possible otherwise for Sassoon to conclude, in this particular instance about the Italian Communist Party (PCI), unwavering as it was in its commitment to parliamentary democracy, that

> ... it remained a party which was on the wrong side of the Cold War divide, and hence a party whose loyalty to the West was in doubt. The others, as long as they were not communists, were 'reliable' - however corrupt (Italian Christian democracy); however illiberal or fascistic (the Greek Colonels, Portugal's António Salazar, Spain's Francisco Franco); however murderous (Chile's Augusto Pinochet or Indonesia's General Suharto).[482]

Countries were judged by the same yardstick, the US measure by which it gauged its interests, often acting on the basis of reflex rather than reflection. The latter came afterwards, if it came at all. As Sassoon continues,

The consequences of considering the communists [and Communism generally] 'unreliable' from the Western democratic point of view were formidable: the struggle against them need not remain confined within the formal rules of liberal democracy, for, to defend freedom, it was argued, it may be necessary to use any weapons, including detestable ones (murder, terrorism, deceit, external interference, bribery).[483]

In their 1996 book Linz and Stepan explore the issues of democratic transition and consolidation, a process that is usually sequential for authoritarian regimes that, whether through choice or pressure, are adopting the democratic model. Of all the countries they consider, they conclude that only Portugal completed both processes at the same time. The transition started with the 1974 revolution but finished the same day as democratic consolidation was achieved - the election in August 1982 when the military accepted the new constitution. They argue that Portugal was also the first to begin the process and therefore had no model to follow (unlike Spain or Greece, for example), though this assertion might be contested by many countries that had to reconstruct themselves in 1945.[484] Portugal's transition had knock-on effects elsewhere, not just in its African colonies.

That Portugal took eight years to complete the process demonstrates the relative nature of transition, with the desired destination of consolidation often a matter of degree. The latter might depend, for example, on the models of governance, the balances within the executive and between the executive and the legislature, the extent of suffrage, and so on. For example, is a system with mid-term elections more or less of a consolidated democracy than one with all-or-nothing elections? Is a presidential system more or less democratic than a parliamentary one? If elections are held at fixed intervals, is this more or less democratic? Does the length of time between elections matter? Is proportional representation fundamental?

There are many other such questions that make it obvious that democracy is a relative rather than absolute concept - or, to put it another way, not all democracies are equally so. Nor should we expect that they will be, just as we do not assume that the authoritarian communist rule practised in Eastern Europe in 1974 is equivalent to the dictatorial, often military, regimes that held sway across much of Latin America at that time. Linz and Stepan differentiate non-democratic regimes into four types, giving examples of each. Of the countries considered in this book, they describe the USSR as totalitarian (but only in the period before Stalin's death in 1953) and Uruguay and Chile as authoritarian. There is no overlap with their post-totalitarian and 'sultanistic' types.[485]

An alternative approach is to consider countries in 1974 along the two dimensions of stability and governance. Table 3 attempts this categorisation. Although this might receive general endorsement, the test is not whether it is in any sense 'correct' but whether it is useful as a way of conceptualising countries in 1974. There may be particularly strong views on the position of the USA, but this reflects both internal difficulties and its support, frequently its enabling, of repressive regimes.

		Degree of Flux	
		Stable	**In transition**
Governance	**Democracy**	Austria Australia Britain Canada France W Germany	Cyprus Northern Ireland Colombia
		United States	
			Vietnam*
	Authoritarian or Dictatorship	USSR Eastern Europe Middle East	Rhodesia Greece Ethiopia Portugal Angola Mozambique Uruguay Chile Bolivia Guatemala

Table 3: Countries in 1974 on governance and flux dimensions
* Vietnam was a special case with both types of governance north and south and in transition to a new state.

One of the implications of this typology is that, while nearly all countries have to pay attention to economic performance, and consequently to economic and business cycles, only democracies are subject to political cycles. In the 1970s many of them had socialist governments with a reaction setting in during the 1980s and a shift to conservative, neo-liberal rule. But not all countries followed this pattern, even in Europe. France, for example, was the reverse, while Austria maintained its socialist approach throughout the 1980s.[486] The equivalent issues for authoritarian regimes might be the extent to which human rights are trampled on, whether this is known or concealed, and whether overt repression is required to keep the populace under control or more subtle means are deployed. For countries in transition, internal security and terrorism can be critical, while for others it might be external influence that is most vital. Superpowers, for example, are particularly attentive to events elsewhere (well beyond the cognisance that all countries have to pay to their neighbours' intentions), but they have to maintain an internal focus as well. Stable democracies may join or form supra-national economic and security organisations to better assure certainty. The EEC (EU) and NATO are the most obvious examples (with COMECON and the Warsaw Pact being established in response).

The world was facing economic crisis in 1974 but for some countries this was a secondary consideration after their own structural turmoil. This makes the situation at the time, and analyses since, far from straightforward. A prominent distinction drawn in 1974 that remains pertinent today is between the *social* market economy (of, for example, West Germany) and the *free* market economy of, for example, the US then and now, and the UK post-Thatcher when the welfare contract between the nation and its people, the human settlement arrived at following the Second World War, was abandoned in all important respects.

The difference of course depends not only on degree but primarily on purpose and motivation. In all economies the state has a role, if only to sweep up those who would otherwise fall through the safety net of health and welfare; in all societies, as JK Galbraith has pointed out, the state has the fundamental duty to plan and commission (if not provide) the basic infrastructure such as roads, hospitals and schools, for example, on which the public's expectation of services depends, even if the services themselves are sometimes delivered by private sector providers. In such instances the extent to which the state regulates, ensuring standards of service are achieved and adhered to, determines whether the society is essentially a social, co-operative one or a free market-dominated one where the interests of investors and rewards to shareholders are paramount. This dichotomy brings with it too the distinction between longer term gains, which the state is concerned with, and the shorter time horizon of immediate pay-offs that individuals concentrate on. To characterise the extremes: the social state is concerned with lasting development that will benefit future generations as well as the current one, whereas private sector capitalism is thinking primarily of the here-and-now, or at best of an individual lifetime only.[487]

But it is not just economies and societies that can be social or free, and all the gradations in between, but so can the people living in those societies. Freedom depends on the ability to exercise choice and so to be homeless, or poor and sick, in the US, perhaps the ultimate definition of a free market economy, is not to be free in any meaningful sense of the term. Similarly, while the tendency might be towards community and co-operation in socially-oriented societies, it is up to each individual to determine the extent of their participation. Being homeless, or otherwise at risk and deprived, offers little consolation no matter how congenial the society might be generally.

According to Patience and Head in their analysis of Australian politics in the 1970s and the growing international economic crisis that provided the context,

> The causes of the world crisis are extraordinarily complex ... aptly described as a 'criss-crossing web of unresolved issues in which the world has suddenly become entangled'.[488]

One might quibble over the use of the word "suddenly" for there was no sound so loud in 1974 as the beating of wings as birds came home to roost, yet they are surely right to identify the oil price rise, the disagreements over market structure of the world's gold system, inflation, increasing unemployment and growing welfare budgets as significant factors. As Butler and Kitzinger put it,

> The year and a half since October 1973 had seen the sharpest break in post-war economic history. The rise in oil prices demonstrated the abject dependence of the world on Middle East suppliers. Food and commodity prices soared. The consequent

balance of payments deficits and monetary disorder affected the Western and developing countries alike.[489]

In Britain the 1970s have been widely described as a 'dismal, benighted decade',[490] and there were shocks to the national and world economies that Britain was ill-prepared for after twenty-five years of post-war growth, but this is perhaps too bleak and too self-serving a judgement for it often derives from a 1980s perspective keen to cast itself in the most positive light. With the benefit of a longer lens, the New Economics Foundation concluded in 2004 that 1976 was Britain's best year since the 1950s on an index of overall well-being.[491]

As Malyn Newitt wrote of the impact of the new 1928 labour code on Portugal's Mozambique colony, "continuity, as so often in history, silently triumphed where change had been so loudly trumpeted".[492] But this is not to say that continuity may not take a different form, hence the focus on the oil resources of Libya, Iraq, Iran and Venezuela since 2000 and the international struggles that have resulted as the west, particularly the US, seeks to maintain access to the supplies on which its economy depends. It is said that the horrendous prospects of climate change, and the protests of the young against this, ensure that the use of fossil fuels (such as oil) is on the way out. That may prove to be the case, but it is far from certain at the time of writing that this is how the future will unwind. There are too many groups in the developed world, and too many economies in the developing world, that have an interest in matters not being turned on their head so precipitately.[493] Not to mention the absence of the basic infrastructure that will be required. Perhaps the Trump wall, rather than deterring immigrants, will prove more valuable in harnessing the wind as an alternative fuel?

This would be the best use to which any new border wall could be put for the evidence from history is that walls (sometimes justified as "peace lines"), whether in Berlin, Cyprus, Northern Ireland or that between Israel and Palestine, divide people and cement conflict and resentment. They not only keep people apart in the short-term but prevent the interaction between them and their communities that are vital to promoting understanding and change. A wall is not only a physical barrier but a psychological impediment to growth, development and progress. A parallel, rather than alternative, view is that walls are such a challenge to the human spirit that their existence demands they are breached. "Don't fence me in," Cole Porter wrote in 1934, a song that has remained in the repertoire from Gene Autry's rendition in 1945 to that of David Byrne (of the band Talking Heads) more recently. In an intellectually richer and more erudite vein, Reilly draws attention to the stress both Alexis de Tocqueville and the Mayan holy book of Guatemala (the Popol Vuh) place on equality as fundamental to civilisation. The Mayan phrase is "let no-one be left behind".[494] You do not get equivalence of conditions and equality between people if there is a wall between them.

What is feasible, though, is that flux in the 21st century will exceed that of the 20th and may prove so great that there is no one left to write about it. Despite all the dangers and prognostications at the time, the writing on the wall in 1974 has been survived. But whether it has been read and understood is another matter. The pursuit of economic growth for its own sake is no longer sustainable nor rational. The opportunity to re-calibrate ambition with social, human aims is upon us - a challenge certainly, but one that the West should face and embrace rather than shirk. In the less developed world, which can compare itself with those countries that offer its residents a better quality of life, the suggestion that growth should be halted is offensive and inappropriate. Why should some people accept less so that those in the northern hemisphere can retain more? This is the colonial slant on history and is long past its sell-by date. 'Growth for its own sake' is entirely irrational, while development of those who lag behind is not only equitable but makes abundant sense in an inter-dependent and globally conscious world.[495]

The existence of supra-national organisations, whether supposedly comprehensive (from the League of Nations to the United Nations) or specific to particular interest groups (from NATO to G7 to OPEC to the Socialist International), demonstrates the recognition of a world that transcends purely national interest. As Morrison put it, "The Portuguese Revolution is but one more piece of evidence attesting to the continuing growth in interdependence among the world's economies today".[496] Not for nothing did Helmut Schmidt publish his 1985 Yale University lectures as 'A Grand Strategy for the West: The Anachronism of National Strategies in an

Interdependent World'. In his opening lecture Schmidt identified four phases in this supposed "Grand Strategy" (foreign, economic, military) of the west from the end of the Second World War: (1) co-operation attempt to 1949; (2) cold war and arms race; (3) co-operation on the basis of assured security, i.e., détente 1967-1976; the peaks being the CSCE conference in Helsinki 1975 and surviving the collapse of the Bretton Woods agreement; and (4) back at cold war and arms race from late 1970s. There is a circularity here that represents the alternation of national interests with global ones. The critical thing might be to break out of this cycle but that requires leaders with vision, energy and determination who are prepared to put aside the short-term in favour of the beneficial objective further off. That goes against much of the drive in the west (financial markets, for example) and is likely to bring down opprobrium on their heads - so they will also require courage. In addition, they will have to be prepared to put aside their interests today, as well as think out of the political and economic box, in favour of tomorrow. That may well be too tall an order, though the world does at least have the advantage today of a common threat that imperils the survival of everybody. Climate change has replaced the nuclear arms race as the only existential threat and certainly the only one that matters. The challenge is to give up the focus on our own backyard and pool our skills and resources collectively. Or are we content to stand by, protecting our narrow sectional interests, while the flux of the past escalates into a future from which there is no escape. Are we able to flex sufficiently and co-operate in the wider, global interest?

Postscript

The foregoing was written before Covid-19 changed the world in early 2020. The commonality with climate change is that both are about human behaviour as if payoffs in the short-term were more important than the long-term consequences. Both Covid-19 and climate change require a co-ordinated international response to tackle them effectively.[497] Yet, even in response to the banking crisis of 2007/08 we struggled to sustain a multilateral stance for very long, though Gordon Brown (UK PM), President Obama (of the US), the G7 and the European Central Bank initiated a common approach that injected liquidity into the banks and protected individual deposits. But both in the UK, and in the International Monetary Fund (IMF)/EU treatment of Greece, insular austerity soon became the preference - with all the damage that resulted for individuals and their families. There should be no doubt that this was ideological preference rather than necessity, and it is illuminating how readily financial resources have been deployed to protect jobs in the Covid crisis. In the UK, for example, after ten years of austerity to reduce borrowing it has leapt to the highest levels outside wartime. Or to put it another way, ten years of unnecessarily blighted lives because of a flawed political ideology modelled on household economics have been rapidly superseded by human values and state intervention that look very close to socialism.

The difference is in the reaction. One response to Covid-19 has been panic, which raises the question 'why?' given that the risk for any individual person is slight. Might the multiplicity of scare stories masquerading as news have changed us from sentient, analytical and discerning beings? Might the pictures from elsewhere have offered a warning of what to expect? Did the changing strategy from the UK government suggest that, in the absence of coherent leadership, it was everyone for themselves? Did the hype on social media generate an equally flailing and desperate response?

Not everyone reacted in the same way of course, with many remaining calm and others proving altruistic. But you only had to visit your nearest supermarket to see how the herd mentality had reasserted itself. Empty shelves testified to the self-interest, regardless of government advice and the effect on others, that many were engaged in. That this is totally irrational made no difference. If everyone carried on as before, there would be sufficient for all. It is being selfish that hastens shortages for everybody and probably leads in the longer term to rationing.

That Covid-19 is far from the first virus to threaten people in the twenty-first century may mean that, rather than change their behaviour, people have become inured to the effects. This is how life now is some may think and, while medical immunity may be achieved eventually (against this virus if not the next), vaccination is mainly social and against how life was in the twentieth century (and could be still).

The contrast with the predominantly calm (or in denial) response to the climate crisis could hardly be more marked, yet that is a far greater and more lasting, less temporary, threat to life as we have known it. The timescale may not be today, but it is tomorrow; individuals can have some impact but real change will only come when societies act responsibly; and it is easier to sublimate (and forget) a crisis that is not staring you in the face each day. To some extent this is how people are programmed to function for it would be difficult to act at all if you focussed on tomorrow's armageddon. Paralysis is not an adaptive strategy. However, without any attention to the possibility of apocalypse, we will guarantee that we get there sooner.

Young people are often the ones who protest against hypocrisy, injustice and inequality in the hope of bringing about change. Frequently, their efforts are dismissed as the 'idealism of youth'. The distressing thing is that we all had that once. As other interests and responsibilities kick in with age, idealism and values are frequently jettisoned in order to protect what we have, vested interests looking after their own. This is not a universal of course, but it is sufficiently widespread to have considerable validity and goes a long way to explaining why young people are often the most vociferous against climate change (they also have the most to lose, a future as well as a past, but that is only part of the reason), while older people voted disproportionately for the island UK, separate from the other 27 EU countries, and are often more submissive in the face of authority and dictatorship.

If ever there was a time for people to say 'enough is enough', this is it. If there is one benefit to have come out of the virus crisis, it is that climate change has been stayed. Whether this is a temporary pause or permanent remission is up to us. This in turn leads to a second possible benefit: the opportunity to re-consider our priorities for the twenty-first century. Put bluntly, the choice is between the pursuit of profit for the few or more equal shares for all and the survival of the planet. Which do we want?

APPENDIX: UN MEMBER COUNTRIES IN 1974 BY CONTINENT

Continent	Country	Year joined UN
Africa	Algeria	1962
	Botswana	1966
	Burundi	1962
	Cameroun	1960
	Central African Republic	1960
	Chad	1960
	Congo (Congo (Brazzaville) to 1971)	1960
	Dahomey (Benin from 1974)	1960
	Egypt (United Arab Republic with Syria from 1958; United Arab Republic - without Syria - from 1961; Egypt from 1971)	1945
	Ethiopia	1945
	Equatorial Guinea	1968
	Gabon	1960
	Gambia	1965
	Ghana	1957
	Guinea	1958
	Guinea-Bissau	1974
	Ivory Coast (Côte d'Ivoire from 1985)	1960
	Kenya	1963
	Lesotho	1966
	Libya	1955
	Malagasy Republic (Madagascar from 1975)	1960
	Malawi	1964
	Mali	1960
	Mauritania	1961
	Mauritius	1968
	Morocco	1956
	Niger	1960
	Nigeria	1960
	Rwanda	1962
	Senegal	1960
	Sierra Leone	1961
	Somalia	1960
	South Africa (Union of South Africa to 1961)	1945
	Sudan	1956
	Swaziland	1968

Continent	Country	Year joined UN
Africa (cont.)	Tanganyika (Tanzania from 1974 with Zanzibar)	1961
	Togo	1960
	Tunisia	1956
	Uganda	1962
	Upper Volta (Burkina Faso from 1984)	1960
	Zaire (Democratic Republic of Congo from 1997)	1960
	Zambia	1964
	Zanzibar (Tanzania from 1974 with Tanganyika)	1963
Asia	Afghanistan	1946
	Bahrain	1971
	Bangladesh	1974
	Bhutan	1971
	Burma	1948
	Cambodia	1955
	Ceylon (Sri Lanka from 1991)	1955
	China	1945
	Democratic Yemen (Yemen from 1990 with Yemen)	1967
	India	1945
	Indonesia	1950
	Iran	1945
	Iraq	1945
	Israel	1949
	Japan	1956
	Jordan	1955
	Kuwait	1963
	Laos	1955
	Lebanon	1945
	Malaysia (Federation of Malaya to 1963)	1957
	Maldive Islands	1965
	Mongolia	1961
	Nepal	1955
	Oman	1971
	Pakistan	1947
	Philippines (Philippine Republic to 1947)	1945
	Qatar	1971
	Saudi Arabia	1945
	Singapore	1965
	Syria	1945

Continent	Country	Year joined UN
Asia (cont.)	(United Arab Republic with Egypt from 1958; Syria from 1961)	
	Thailand (Siam to 1949)	1946
	United Arab Emirates	1971
	Yemen (Yemen from 1990 with Democratic Yemen)	1947
Europe	Albania	1955
	Austria	1955
	Belgium	1945
	Bulgaria	1955
	Byelorussian Soviet Socialist Republic (Belarus from 1991)	1945
	Cyprus	1960
	Czechoslovakia (Czech Republic and Slovakia from 1993)	1945
	Denmark	1945
	Federal Republic of Germany (Germany from 1990)	1973
	Finland	1955
	France	1945
	German Democratic Republic (Germany from 1990)	1973
	Greece	1945
	Hungary	1955
	Iceland	1946
	Ireland	1955
	Italy	1955
	Luxembourg	1945
	Malta	1964
	Netherlands	1945
	Norway	1945
	Poland	1945
	Portugal	1955
	Romania	1955
	Spain	1955
	Sweden	1946
	Turkey	1945
	Ukrainian Soviet Socialist Republic (Ukraine from 1991)	1945
	Union of Soviet Socialist Republics (Russian Federation from 1991; 11 other countries in Commonwealth of Independent States from 1991/92)	1945
	United Kingdom	1945
	Yugoslavia	1945

Continent	Country	Year joined UN
Europe (cont.)	(Bosnia and Herzegovina, Croatia, and Slovenia from 1992; Macedonia from 1993; Yugoslavia from 2000, then Serbia and Montenegro from 2003 and each separately from 2006)	
North America	Bahamas	1973
	Barbados	1966
	Canada	1945
	Costa Rica	1945
	Cuba	1945
	Dominican Republic	1945
	El Salvador	1945
	Grenada	1974
	Guatemala	1945
	Haiti	1945
	Honduras	1945
	Jamaica	1962
	Mexico	1945
	Nicaragua	1945
	Panama	1945
	Trinidad and Tobago	1962
	United States	1945
(Australia and) Oceania	Australia	1945
	Fiji	1970
	New Zealand	1945
South America (with addition of Suriname from 1975)	Argentina	1945
	Bolivia	1945
	Brazil	1945
	Chile	1945
	Colombia	1945
	Ecuador	1945
	French Guiana (see France)	
	Guyana	1966
	Paraguay	1945
	Peru	1945
	Suriname (see Netherlands)	
	Uruguay	1945
	Venezuela	1945

* https://www.un.org/en/sections/member-states/growth-united-nations-membership-1945-present/index.html - accessed 31st May 2019

NOTES

Acknowledgements p. iv
[1] *Liverpool Echo* 27th December 1974
[2] *Birmingham Daily Post* 24th January and 14th February 1974

Calendar of Events [pp. vii-xi]
[3] Selected from the Chronicle of Events in the 'Annual Register of World Events' for 1974

Chapter 1 pp1-8
[4] Organisation for Economic Co-operation and Development (OECD) statistics show an annual decrease in GDP per head in seven of twenty-six member countries in 1974 and in sixteen, more than half the members, in 1975. Four countries showed decreases in both years (UK, USA, Denmark and Portugal).
https://stats.oecd.org/Index.aspx?DatasetCode=SNA_TABLE1# -accessed 14th January 2020
[5] Barbara Castle, 'The Castle Diaries 1974-1976', 1980, p62
[6] The second three-day week and the third state of emergency declared by the Conservative government, according to Barbara Castle. 'Castle Diaries', p1
[7] They were never activated.
[8] Ben Pimlott, 'Harold Wilson', 1992, p607
[9] Kenneth Maxwell, 'The Making of Portuguese Democracy', 1995
[10] Latin American Bureau Special Brief, 'Uruguay: Generals Rule', 1980, p53
[11] 'Crude but shrewd' as Keith Brace put it in his *Birmingham Daily Post* report in February 1974.
[12] JLS Girling, "Indo-China", pp12-13 in Mohammed Ayoob (ed.), 'Conflict and Intervention in the Third World', 1980
[13] Denis Healey, 'The Time of My Life', 1990 (orig. 1989), p371
[14] Harold Wilson, 'Final Term: The Labour Government 1974-1976', 1979, p20
[15] https://www.un.org/en/sections/member-states/growth-united-nations-membership-1945-present/index.html - accessed 31st May 2019
[16] Raymond L Garthoff, 'Détente and Confrontation: American-Soviet Relations from Nixon to Reagan', 1985, pp360-408
[17] Ibid, p383
[18] Ibid, p396

Chapter 2 pp9-17
[19] Quoted in Philip Short, 'Mitterand: A Study in Ambiguity', 2013, p158
[20] Ibid, p157
[21] Wilson, op cit, p107
[22] David Butler and Uwe Kitzinger, 'The 1975 Referendum', 1976, p15

[23] Ibid, p6

[24] Ibid, p16

[25] Wilson, op cit, p55

[26] Ibid, p90

[27] Tony Benn, 'Against the Tide: Diaries 1973-1976', 1990 (orig. 1989), p2

[28] Kenneth O Morgan, 'Callaghan: A Life', 1997, p385
The shadow Cabinet majority were "Wilson, Callaghan, Foot, Benn, Mulley, Shore, Short, and Mellish, with the mainly pro-European group of Shirley Williams, Lever, Crosland, Houghton, Thompson and Jenkins on the other side".

[29] Cited in Melissa Pine, 'Harold Wilson and Europe: Pursuing Britain's Membership of the European Community', 2012, pp17 & 157
Robert Saunders, 'Yes to Europe: The 1975 Referendum and Seventies Britain', 2018, p61 also makes this point.

[30] Wilson, op cit, pp94-95

[31] Peter Shore had pointed out to Benn on 9th May 1974 that he expected the European Community to "take a very different direction as a result". Benn, op cit, p150

[32] Butler and Kitzinger, op cit, p31

[33] Ibid, p33

[34] Wilson, op cit, p96

[35] Ibid, p93

[36] Ibid, p101

[37] Butler and Kitzinger, op cit, p45

[38] Saunders, op cit, p61

[39] Wilson, op cit, pp103-105

[40] Ibid, p108

[41] https://blogs.lse.ac.uk/brexit/2019/08/20/the-risks-of-simple-majority-referendums-learning-from-quebec/ - accessed 24th January 2020

[42] Wilson, op cit, p101

[43] Although Qualified Majority Voting is now used in about 80% of EU Council votes, unanimity is still required in 'sensitive' areas - i.e., those that that might be most relevant to issues of national sovereignty. see https://www.consilium.europa.eu/en/council-eu/voting-system/unanimity/ - accessed 18th August 2020

[44] Joe Haines, 'Glimmers of Twilight: Harold Wilson in Decline', 2003, p41

[45] Pimlott, op cit, p659

[46] Peter Jenkins, *Guardian* 14th March 1975

[47] Helene Miard-Delacroix, 'Willy Brandt: Life of a Statesman', 2016, pp136-137. However, this may be hindsight.

Chapter 3 pp19-30

[48] James Ker-Lindsay, 'The Cyprus Problem', 2011, p. xvi points out, as do many others, that to Turkey and the Turkish Cypriots it was an 'intervention' or 'peace operation', but to the Greek Cypriots an 'invasion'.

[49] Peter Godwin and Ian Hancock, 'Rhodesians Never Die: The Impact of War and Political Change on White Rhodesia c1970-1980', 1993, p87

[50] The Treaty of Alliance permitted Greece and Turkey to maintain small military forces (Greece 950 and Turkey 650 troops max.) on the island and to work together with Cyprus on its defence. The Treaty of Establishment allowed Britain to maintain its existing bases as sovereign territory (99 square miles in total) and access to some other facilities.

[51] NM Ertekun, 'The Cyprus Dispute and the Birth of the Turkish Republic of Northern Cyprus', 2nd edition, 1984 (orig. 1981), pp8-11

[52] Clement H Dodd, 'The Cyprus Issue: A Current Perspective', 1994, p7

[53] Ertekun, op cit, pp31-33

[54] Ibid, pp34-35

[55] William Mallinson, 'Cyprus, A Modern History', 2005, p84

[56] Ibid, p85

[57] John Reddaway, 'Burdened with Cyprus: The British Connection', 1986, p167

[58] Christopher Hitchens, 'Cyprus', 1984, pp137-138

[59] Dodd, op cit, p6

[60] Mallinson, op cit, p77

[61] Ibid, p85

[62] Ibid, p75

[63] Garthoff, op cit, p415 described this as the first major defeat for Kissinger "and for the new Ford administration. The Soviets were not involved."

[64] Ian Hancock, "Rhodesia", p178 in Mohammed Ayoob (ed.), 'Conflict and Intervention in the Third World', 1980

[65] Martin Meredith, 'The Past is Another Country: Rhodesia 1890-1979', 1979, p144

[66] Ian Hancock, 'White Liberals, Moderates and Radicals in Rhodesia: 1953-1980', 1984, p193

[67] Meredith, op cit, p134

[68] Godwin & Hancock, op cit, p103

[69] Ibid, p119

[70] Ibid, p106

[71] http://pitts.emory.edu/collections/digitalcollections/exhibits/political-cartoons.cfm - accessed 26th March 2020
"The scene in an imaginary caravan lot … is an indirect criticism of government policy of moving whole communities from their homes in Tribal Trust Lands, i.e., African communal lands."

[72] Meredith, op cit, p150

[73] Ibid, p154

[74] Godwin & Hancock, op cit, p118

[75] Ken Flower, 'Serving Secretly: Rhodesia's CIO Chief on Record', 1987, p159

[76] Godwin & Hancock, op cit, pp118 & 122

[77] Castle, op cit, p245

[78] Godwin & Hancock, op cit, p130

[79] Meredith, op cit, p132

[80] Godwin & Hancock, op cit, p108

[81] Paul Bew and Gordon Gillespie, 'Northern Ireland: A Chronology of the Troubles 1968-1993', 1993, pp40 & 60

[82] Jack Holland, 'Hope Against History: The Ulster Conflict', 1999, pp105-106

[83] Compiled from the annual totals in Bew and Gillespie, op cit

[84] Patrick Buckland, 'A History of Northern Ireland', 1981, p124; Bew & Gillespie, op cit, p7

[85] Buckland, op cit, pp122-123

[86] Bew & Gillespie, op cit, pp3-4

[87] Jim McBride, "Civil rights 1968 and Northern Ireland", *The Historian*, Winter 2018-19, 140, pp8-12

[88] Buckland, op cit, p105

[89] Buckland, op cit, pp138-140; Bew & Gillespie, op cit, pp25 & 32

[90] Buckland, op cit, pp167-168

[91] Bew & Gillespie, op cit, pp78-83 & 88

[92] Buckland, op cit, pp144 & 173

[93] https://www.britannica.com/topic/Good-Friday-Agreement

Chapter 4 pp31-45

[94] "Portugal was both the first European nation to colonise Africa [in the fifteenth century] and virtually the last to leave". See James Ciment, 'Angola and Mozambique: Postcolonial Wars in Southern Africa', 1997, pp35-36

[95] Noam Chomsky, 'Deterring Democracy', 1992 (orig. 1991), p99 re Michael Mandelbaum, "Ending the Cold War", *Foreign Affairs*, Spring 1989

[96] http://academic.brooklyn.cuny.edu/history/johnson/clark.htm - accessed 2nd August 2019

[97] https://www.cia.gov/library/readingroom/docs/CIA-RDP85T00287R000400320001-4.pdf - accessed 2nd August 2019

[98] John Stockwell, 'In Search of Enemies: A CIA Story', 1978, p10

[99] John W Harbeson, 'The Ethiopian Transformation: The Quest for the Post-Imperial State', 1988, p23

[100] http://addisstandard.com/news-ethiopian-authorities-deport-prominent-scholar-rene-lefort-from-airport-no-explanation/ - accessed 31st July 2019

[101] René Lefort, 'Ethiopia: An Heretical Revolution?', 1983 (orig. 1981)

[102] Ibid, p48

[103] Edmond J Keller, 'Revolutionary Ethiopia: From Empire to People's Republic', 1991, p167

[104] Ibid, p168

[105] https://www.youtube.com/watch?v=ML32CeRUgIU - accessed 31st July 2019

[106] Keller, op cit, pp169-170; Harbeson, op cit, p85

[107] Lefort, op cit, p49

[108] Ibid, p3

[109] Keller, op cit, pp138-140

[110] Martin Meredith, 'The State of Africa: A History of Fifty Years of Independence', 2005, pp206-217

[111] Keller, op cit, pp171-172; Harbeson, op cit, p89 details the scale of these.

[112] Keller, op cit, pp173-174

[113] Ibid, pp176-178

[114] Ibid, pp181-184

[115] Lefort, op cit, pp69 & 80

[116] Similar examples (e.g., for women and minorities, not to say immigrants) can be seen in Trump's America in 2019 where 'America First' provides equivalent justification.

[117] Harbeson, op cit, p3

[118] Karl Meier, 'Angola: Promises and Lies', 1996, p16

[119] Inge Tvedten, 'Angola: Struggle for Peace and Reconstruction', 1997, p29

[120] Ciment, op cit, p12

[121] Ibid, p39

[122] Tvedten, op cit, p31

[123] Such settlements were also implemented in Mozambique where the Portuguese colonial authority judged them the best way of "insulating the population from FRELIMO propaganda". These aldeamentos, as they were called, developed further after independence for the Frelimo government adopted them as key to its policy of rural development. Malyn Newitt, 'A History of Mozambique', 1995, p473

[124] Tvedten, op cit, p32

[125] Newitt, op cit, p530

[126] Ciment, op cit, p39

[127] Ibid, p41

[128] Ibid, p47

[129] Ibid, pp48-49

[130] Ibid, p50

[131] Stockwell, op cit, p48

[132] Tony Hodges, 'Angola from Afro-Stalinism to Petro-Diamond Capitalism', 2001, p10

[133] Ciment, op cit, p14

[134] Newitt, op cit, p522; Iain Christie, 'Machel of Mozambique', 1988, pp19-22

[135] Newitt, op cit, p522

[136] Ibid, p517

[137] Ibid, p533

[138] Ibid, p495

[139] Christie, op cit, pp8-9

[140] Newitt, op cit, p477

[141] Christie, op cit, p7

[142] Ibid, p13

[143] Newitt, op cit, p523; Christie, op cit, p32

[144] Newitt, op cit, pp524-532

[145] Ibid, p537

[146] Ibid, p538

[147] Ibid, pp539-540

[148] Ciment, op cit, pp64-65 See Christie, op cit, pp26-27 for examples of shared sacrifices.

[149] Ciment, op cit, pp64-65

[150] https://www.aljazeera.com/news/2019/08/mozambique-president-renamo-leader-sign-peace-deal-190801115411693.html - accessed 14th August 2019

[151] Newitt, op cit, p472

[152] Gabriel Kolko, 'Anatomy of a War: Vietnam, the US and Modern Historical Experience', 1994 (orig. 1985), pp461 & 462

[153] Ibid, p489

[154] Kissinger and Le Duc Tho were jointly awarded the Nobel peace prize. Kissinger accepted but Tho refused, noting that true peace did not yet exist in Vietnam.

[155] Garthoff, op cit, p259

[156] Kolko, op cit, p472

[157] Ibid, pp463-468

[158] Ibid, pp474-475

[159] Ibid, pp476-477

Chapter 5 pp47-52

[160] http://www.censusscope.org/us/chart_popl.html and https://www.cia.gov/library/readingroom/docs/CIA-RDP85T00875R001900010212-2.pdf - both accessed 11th June 2019

[161] https://www.nytimes.com/2017/12/20/us/pentagon-papers-post.html - accessed 11th June 2019

[162] Louis Liebovich, 'Richard Nixon, Watergate and the Press: A Historical Retrospective', 2003, pp ix, 17 & 107

[163] Liebovich makes the point that "The *Washington Post* kept the story alive [in 1972 and 1973], but television and the Watergate hearings drove the president from office." Ibid, p119

[164] Fred Emery, 'Watergate: The Corruption and Fall of Richard Nixon', 1974, pp39-73 also reports on the administration's extreme reaction to the publication of the Pentagon Papers.

[165] Liebovich, op cit, pp35-39

[166] Ibid, pp1-19

[167] Ibid, p24

[168] Ibid, pp53-54

[169] Ibid, p73

[170] This was actually the second break-in by the plumbers who were rectifying malfunctioning wiretaps they had placed three weeks earlier (on 27th May) and installing additional ones.

[171] Liebovich, op cit, p66

[172] Ibid, p77

[173] Ibid, pp83 & 85

[174] Garthoff, op cit, p416

[175] This was the same day the Arab-Israeli Yom Kippur started and must have multiplied Nixon's problems.

[176] Garthoff, op cit, p415

[177] Ibid, p435

[178] Liebovich, op cit, p106

[179] Ibid, p111

[180] Garthoff, op cit, p436

Chapter 6 pp53-61

[181] Daniel Möckli, 'European Foreign Policy During the Cold War: Heath, Brandt, Pompidou and the Dream of Political Unity', 2009, p120

[182] June 1975 speech, "America: You must think about the world", in Alexander Solzhenitsyn, 'Détente: Prospects for Democracy and Dictatorship', 1976, p19

[183] Ibid

[184] https://www.theguardian.com/world/2019/sep/23/raoul-wallenberg-family-of-diplomat-who-saved-hungarian-jews - accessed 24th September 2019

[185] Keith Brace, "Solzhenitsyn and the politics of dissidence", *Birmingham Daily Post* January 1974

[186] See Sidney Bloch and Peter Reddaway, 'Russia's Political Hospitals: The Abuse of Psychiatry in the Soviet Union', 1977

[187] Joshua Rubenstein, 'Soviet Dissidents: Their Struggle for Human Rights', 1981, p138

[188] Laurie P Salitan, 'Politics and Nationality in Contemporary Soviet-Jewish Emigration, 1965-1989', 1992, p49

[189] https://www.census.gov/content/dam/Census/library/publications/1991/demo/ussr.pdf - accessed 19th September 2019

[190] Charles Gati, 'The Bloc That Failed: Soviet-East European Relations in Transition', 1990, p24

[191] Martin McCauley, "The GDR and the Soviet Union", pp147-165 in David Childs (ed.), 'Honecker's Germany', 1975, p158

[192] Ibid

[193] Avril Pittman, 'From Ostpolitik to Reunification: West German-Soviet Political Relations Since 1974', 1992, pp xi & 9

[194] Ibid, p10

Internal difficulties increased over the pace of *Ostpolitik* and relations with other Communist neighbours by 1974. For example, Gerard Braunthal, 'The West German Social Democrats, 1969-1982: Profile of a Party in Power', 1983, pp11 & 12; Miard-Delacroix, op cit, pp104-107

[195] Until changes to the GDR constitution came into effect in October 1974 it had included the goal of eventual reunification. McCauley, op cit, p160

[196] Möckli, op cit, p106

[197] Ibid, p11

[198] Pimlott, op cit, p669

[199] Rubenstein, op cit, pp28-29

Rubenstein says that "his conduct ... produced difficulties". That is too bland and a misleading assessment of the consequences.

[200] William Tompson, 'The Soviet Union Under Brezhnev', 2003, pp27 & 31

[201] Ibid, p21

[202] Ibid, p39

[203] The Warsaw Pact had been formed in 1955 as a response to West Germany joining NATO.

[204] McCauley, op cit, p159

[205] https://www.nytimes.com/1974/01/30/archives/brezhnev-hailed-by-castro-in-cubaa-soviet-leader-told-cubans-will.html - accessed 2nd August 2019

[206] Rubenstein, op cit, pp81 & 87

[207] The *New York Times* had noted the impact of Watergate on Nixon's ability to conduct foreign policy on 10th April 1974. For example, USSR leaders, regardless of whether they supported Nixon personally, would be wary of any agreements that required Congressional approval. Garthoff, op cit, p424

[208] Ibid, p410

[209] Ibid, p431

[210] Ibid, pp412 & 425

[211] Tompson, op cit, p48

[212] https://www.csce.gov/about-csce/helsinki-process-and-osce - accessed 4th September 2019

The Conference became the Organization for Security and Cooperation in Europe from January 1995, with 57 member states following the break-up of the Soviet Union.

[213] Niall Ferguson, Charles S Maier, Erez Manela & Daniel J Sargent (eds.), 'The Shock of the Global: The 1970s in Perspective', 2010, p347 in Matthew Connelly chapter "Future shock: The end of the world as they knew it", pp337-350.

[214] Tompson, op cit, p48

[215] Quoted in Rubenstein, op cit, p129

[216] In Ferguson et al., op cit, Michael Cotey Morgan argues this in "The seventies and the rebirth of human rights", pp237-250 (p238)

[217] Rubenstein, op cit, p183

Chapter 7 pp63-83

[218] Donald Sassoon, 'One Hundred Years of Socialism: The West European Left in the Twentieth Century', 2019 (orig. 1996) pp461-468
Sassoon covers the period 1970-1989.

[219] Where steady = change of less than 4 percentage points across general elections in decade; there were only two such elections in France, Greece, Norway and Spain.

[220] Compiled from Sassoon, p463
Main party of the Left: Socialist Party in Austria, Spain, Portugal and France; Labour Party in Norway, UK and Holland; Social Democratic Party in Denmark, Finland, Sweden and West Germany; Communist Party in Italy; Walloon and Flemish parties in Belgium

[221] Short, op cit, p292
Short further explains that the "Italian and Spanish Communists had condemned their Portuguese comrades" but, as the French Communists under Marchais had not, Mitterand was also criticising them.

[222] Sassoon, op cit, p581
Berlinguer allied himself with the French and Spanish communists to bring about "the birth of 'Eurocommunism', an attempt to map out a new path for European communism based on a firm commitment to the values of parliamentary democracy. [It] would not survive the increasingly erratic behaviour of the French, and the eccentricities of the then Spanish leader, Santiago Carrillo."

[223] A referendum in 2000 reduced each term to five years.

[224] https://www.un.org/en/sections/member-states/growth-united-nations-membership-1945-present/index.html - accessed 31st May 2019

[225] Ian Kershaw, 'Roller-Coaster: Europe 1950-2017', 2018, pp263 & 293

[226] Beate Kohler, 'Political Forces in Spain, Greece and Portugal', 1982, preface

[227] https://www.nato.int/cps/en/natohq/topics_52044.htm - accessed 8th October 2019

[228] Helmut Schmidt, 'A Grand Strategy for the West: The Anachronism of National Strategies in an Interdependent World', 1985
The chapters in this book started out in 1985 as Schmidt's Stimson lectures at Yale University.

[229] Kohler, op cit, p108
Richard Clogg, 'A Concise History of Greece', 1992, p171 renders the slogan as 'Karamanlis or the tanks'.
Karamanlis is recorded as denying it in CM Woodhouse, 'Karamanlis: The Restorer of Greek Democracy', 1982, p234

[230] Quoted in Woodhouse, op cit, p168

[231] Ibid, p163

[232] Ibid, p163

[233] Clogg, op cit, pp145 & 150

[234] Letter 9th December 1963 cited in Stan Draneos, 'The "Karamanlis Solution" and the Crisis of 1965-1967', https://sites.google.com/site/standraenos/the-karamanlis-solution-and-the-crisis-of-1965-1967 - accessed 9th October 2019

[235] Woodhouse, op cit, pp176-181

[236] A service or caretaker government was the traditional approach in Greece to avoid the party in power entering the election at an advantage.

[237] Roger Silverman, 'Defiance: Greece and Europe', 2016, p53 and others.

[238] https://www.ahistoryofgreece.com/junta.htm - accessed 9th October 2019

[239] Kohler, op cit, p98

[240] Silverman, op cit, p59

[241] Clogg, op cit, p164

[242] Kershaw, op cit, pp294-295

[243] Clogg, op cit, p165; Woodhouse, op cit, pp197-199

[244] Woodhouse, op cit, p199

[245] Clogg, op cit, p167; Woodhouse, op cit, p201

[246] Thirty-nine in official estimates according to Silverman, op cit, p65

[247] Clogg, op cit, p168

[248] Kohler, op cit, p99

[249] Woodhouse, op cit, pp207-208

[250] Ibid, p208

[251] *Times* 26th July 1974

[252] Kohler, op cit, p99

[253] Woodhouse, op cit, p214; Silverman, op cit, p69

[254] Kohler, op cit, p146

[255] John S Koliopoulos and Thanos M Veremis, 'Greece: The Modern Sequel from 1821 to the Present', 2002, p310

[256] Clogg, op cit, pp175-178

[257] Short, op cit, p280

[258] Ian Derbyshire, 'Politics in France: From Giscard to Mitterand', 1990, p36

[259] Ibid, p34

[260] AM El-Mokadem, D Hawdon, C Robinson and PJ Stevens, 'OPEC and the World Oil Market 1973-1983', 1984, p30

[261] Short, op cit, p280
Kershaw, op cit, p290 adds that "After 1974 the pattern familiar from elsewhere set in. Inflation [in France] rose to over 15 per cent, while unemployment doubled to a million and growth plummeted to minus 0.3 per cent."

[262] https://stats.oecd.org/Index.aspx?DatasetCode=SNA_TABLE1# - accessed 14th January 2020

[263] Kershaw, op cit, pp286-287

[264] Short, op cit, p280

[265] Derbyshire, op cit, p37

[266] Ibid, pp39-42

[267] Ibid, p43

[268] Ibid, pp38-39

[269] Ibid, p53

[270] Stuart Parkes, 'Understanding Contemporary Germany', 1997, p29

[271] Ibid, p21

[272] Ibid, p29

[273] Barbara Marshall, 'Makers of the Twentieth Century: Willy Brandt', 1990, pp85-86

[274] Braunthal, op cit, p248

[275] Miard-Delacroix, op cit, pp152-153

[276] Braunthal, op cit, p11

[277] Helmut Kohl ten years later is the only other example of a Chancellor seeking deliberate defeat through this mechanism in order to trigger an early election. https://www.bundesverfassungsgericht.de/SharedDocs/Entscheidungen/EN/2005/08/es20050825_2bve000405en.html - accessed 6th November 2019

[278] Braunthal, op cit, p273

[279] Gordon Smith, William E Paterson & Peter H Merkl (eds), 'Developments in West German Politics', 1989, pp61-62

[280] Brandt had visited de Gaulle in Paris in April 1962 when he was already being spoken of as a future Chancellor. "De Gaulle had asked to see Brandt again on his official trip to the FRG in September 1962, but the General ... refused to go to Berlin as long as the wall was in place." Miard-Delacroix, op cit, p78

[281] Miard-Delacroix, op cit, pp118-119 & 163 The Treaty of Moscow had been signed 12th August 1970 by Brandt and Brezhnev.

[282] Smith et al., op cit, p70

[283] Kershaw, op cit, p289

[284] Jonathan Carr, 'Helmut Schmidt: Helmsman of Germany', 1985, p101

[285] Kristina Spohr, 'The Global Chancellor: Helmut Schmidt and the Reshaping of the International Order', 2016, pp1 & 6 Braunthal, op cit, pp62-71 & 224, 235 also compares the strengths and weaknesses of Brandt and Schmidt.

[286] https://www.willy-brandt-biography.com/politics/socialist-international/ - accessed 13th November 2019

[287] http://www.brandt21forum.info/About_BrandtCommission.htm - accessed 13th November 2019 These two reports "give primary emphasis to the international issues of food and agricultural development, aid, energy, trade, international monetary and financial reform, and global negotiations. The Brandt

Reports also sought solutions to other problems common to both North and South, including the environment, the arms race, population growth, and the uncertain prospects of the global economy. Since these problems ultimately concern the survival of all nations, the Brandt Commission's recommendations were presented as a structural program to address the world's problems collectively."

[288] Braunthal, op cit, pp284-285

[289] Ibid, p274

[290] Maxwell, op cit, p66

[291] https://stats.oecd.org/Index.aspx?DatasetCode=SNA_TABLE1# - accessed 14th January 2020

[292] Rodney J Morrison, 'Portugal: Revolutionary Change in an Open Society', 1981, p1

[293] Ibid, p14

[294] Pimlott, op cit, p669

[295] Morrison, op cit, p20

[296] Hans Janitschek, 'Mario Soares: Portrait of a Hero', 1985, p48

[297] *Times* 3rd May 1974

[298] Morrison, op cit, p21

[299] Maxwell, op cit, p107

[300] Silverman, op cit, p76

[301] *Times* 25th April 1975

[302] Kershaw, op cit, p298

[303] Morrison, op cit, p34

[304] Ibid, pp33-36

[305] Kershaw, op cit, p298

[306] They included Harold Wilson and James Callaghan from Britain, Willy Brandt and Helmut Schmidt from West Germany, Francois Mitterand from France, Bettino Craxi from Italy, Joop den Uyl from the Netherlands, Bruno Kreisky from Austria, Yitzhak Rabin from Israel, with Olof Palme of Sweden in the chair. Soares was also there.

[307] Morgan, op cit, p432

[308] Ibid, pp442-443

Chapter 8 pp85-93

[309] Though Reykjavik in Iceland is further away at over 1800 miles.

[310] Peter J Katzenstein, 'Corporatism and Change: Austria, Switzerland and the Politics of Industry', 1984, p19

[311] "Their own kind of crusade" survey in *Economist* 28th July 1973, p3

[312] Katzenstein, op cit, p49

[313] Andrew Shonfield, 'Modern Capitalism: The Changing Balance of Public and Private Power', 1965, p193

[314] Katzenstein, op cit, p49

[315] *Proporz* is the usual term for the Austrian system of political control. In other words, that the two main political parties at this time (the Socialists

and the Austrian People's Party or ÖVP) share. See Shonfield, op cit, p193.

This had its drawbacks as well, of course, as Shonfield goes on to point out: "unmitigated party democracy throughout the public sector" had the effect of downgrading the role of Parliament.

[316] Katzenstein, op cit, p10

[318] Shonfield, op cit, p194

[319] Katzenstein, op cit, pp32 & 37

[320] Ibid, pp30 & 33

[321] Steven Beller, 'A Concise History of Austria', 2006, p277

[322] Ibid, p278

[323] Barbara Jelavich, 'Modern Austria: Empire and Republic, 1815-1986', 1987, p316

[324] Beller, op cit, p260

[325] See https://europa.eu/european-union/about-eu/countries_en#tab-0-1 and https://www.austria.org/austria-in-the-eu - both accessed 16th December 2019

[326] In 1974 Kirchschläger was elected President of Austria and was re-elected unopposed in 1980. Jelavich, op cit, p302

[327] Beller, op cit, p275; Jelavich, op cit, p301

[328] Jelavich, op cit, p311

[329] John Fitzmaurice, 'Austrian Politics and Society Today: In Defence of Austria', 1991, pp3, 74-75

[330] Katzenstein, op cit, p38

[331] Ibid, p23

Sassoon, op cit, p469 indicates that Switzerland also had a commitment to full employment (as well as price stability). However, this was of a special sort: "…unemployment in Switzerland was low mainly because the majority of workers who lost their jobs were foreigners on temporary permits who were forced to leave the country once they became unemployed. In effect, Switzerland exported its unemployment. Foreign workers were thus the chief victims of the harsh deflation which allowed Switzerland to weather the oil shock."

[332] *Economist* survey, 28th July 1973, p11

[333] Ibid, p4

[334] Katzenstein, op cit, p48

[335] Ibid, p41

[336] Kreisky foreword in Fitzmaurice, op cit, pxi

[337]

https://fraser.stlouisfed.org/files/docs/historical/federal%20reserve%20hist ory/Stagflation_051979.pdf - accessed 30th December 2019

[338] Jelavich, op cit, p299 Also, Beller, op cit, p273

[339] Katzenstein, op cit, pp68-69 notes that the government sat on the Prices Sub-Committee (started 1957) but did not vote, did not even sit on the Wages Sub-Committee (started 1962), while the third concentrated on

evidence-based expert reports (the Advisory Council for Social and Economic Affairs started 1963).

[340] Ibid, p65

[341] Ibid, p72

[342] Fitzmaurice, op cit, p1

[343] Beller, op cit, p273

Chapter 9 pp95-114

[344] Edy Kaufman, 'Uruguay in Transition: From Civilian to Military Rule', 1979, p14; Nathaniel Davis, 'The Last Two Years of Salvador Allende', 1985, p114

[345] Population in 1974 was estimated at 2.824 million, according to https://www.populationpyramid.net/uruguay/1974/ - accessed 20th February 2020

[346] In support of this, Luis González, 'Political Structures and Democracy in Uruguay', 1991, p3 notes that the male voting age had been 18 in Uruguay since 1918 but only since 1970 in Chile. Similarly, women had voted in Uruguay since 1934 but only since 1952 in Chile.

[347] Martin Weinstein, 'Uruguay: The Politics of Failure', 1975, p xiii

[348] Ibid, pp23-24

[349] Ibid, p xvi

[350] Ibid, p xv

[351] Kaufman, op cit, p31

[352] González, op cit, pp41-42

[353] https://www.theguardian.com/world/2011/jul/19/juan-maria-bordaberry-obituary - accessed 5th February 2020

[354] González, op cit, p35 González adds that between 1930 and 1936 only Colombia (which was not a democracy then) remained stable.

[355] Kaufman, op cit, p ix

[356] Ibid, p xii

[357] Ibid, p40

[358] Ibid, p1

[359] González, op cit, p38 Out of 135 nations only Malawi and the Dominican Republic had a lower growth rate between 1961 and 1965 than Uruguay (-0.9%).

[360] Martin Weinstein, 'Uruguay: Democracy at the Crossroads', 1988, p36

[361] In addition, Kaufman, op cit, pp23-25 confirms that inflation, the cost of living, wages and the rate at which the peso was devalued all increased, while meat exports reduced.

[362] Charles Gillespie, 'Negotiating Democracy: Politicians and Generals in Uruguay', 1991, p38

[363] González, op cit, p39

[364] Ibid, p42

[365] Gillespie, op cit, p33

[366] Ibid

[367] Kaufman, op cit, p26

[368] Ibid, pp22-23

[369] https://www.theguardian.com/news/2004/aug/14/guardianobituaries - accessed 13th February 2020

[370] 'Human Rights in Uruguay and Paraguay: Hearings Before the Sub-Committee on International Organisations of the Committee on International Relations, House of Representatives. June, July and August 1976', Washington, US Government Printing Office, 1976
https://books.google.co.uk/books?id=PepgxVkkinIC&pg=PP3&lpg=PP3&dq=%22Edy+Kaufman%22+AND+%22Martin+Weinstein%22&source=bl&ots=91o7sjxImc&sig=ACfU3U3yo2TtggmoaFNaLyIMMKeT8LmWZA&hl=en&sa=X&ved=2ahUKEwj_-e2z_7nnAhVUnVwKHenjDBQQ6AEwAHoECAgQAQ#v=onepage&q=%22Edy%20Kaufman%22%20AND%20%22Martin%20Weinstein%22&f=false - accessed 5th February 2020
Their testimonies and statements are on pp2-30, 32-36, 36-74, 91-105

[371] Gillespie, op cit, p43

[372] *Times* 25th September 1974
It is worth noting how rarely any British newspapers carried reports of Uruguay in 1974 (other than their performance in the World Cup football tournament held in West Germany).

[373] Kaufman, op cit, p33

[374] https://www.theguardian.com/news/2004/aug/14/guardianobituaries - accessed 13th February 2020

[375] https://www.amnesty.org/download/Documents/204000/amr520131979en.pdf, pp4-5 - accessed 13th February 2020

[376] https://www.odi.org/sites/odi.org.uk/files/odi-assets/publications-opinion-files/6827.pdf, p42 - accessed 13th February 2020

[377] Stephen Gregory, 'Intellectuals and Left Politics in Uruguay 1958-2006', 2009, p79

[378] Weinstein, 1988 op cit, p84

[379] https://www.populationpyramid.net/chile/1974/ - accessed 20th February 2020

[380] UN 2018 figures give 87.5% of the Chilean population living in Santiago, 95% of the Uruguayan in Montevideo. Uruguay has always had the higher urban population (and the highest in South America, where it was 84% in 1981 according to González, op cit, p3).

[381] William Columbus Davis, 'Warnings from the Far South: Democracy versus Dictatorship in Uruguay, Argentina and Chile', 1995, p5

[382] Nathaniel Davis, op cit, p109

[383] Arturo Valenzuela chapter on Chile p185 in Larry Diamond, Juan Linz and Seymour Lipset (eds.), 'Democracy in Developing Countries - vol. 4: Latin America', 1989; Nathaniel Davis, op cit p111

[384] Nathaniel Davis, op cit, pp114-136

[385] *Wall Street Journal* 24th July 1973 quoted in Kaufman, op cit, p49

[386] Juan Linz and Alfred Stepan, 'Problems of Democratic Transition and Consolidation: Southern Europe, South America and Post-Communist Europe', 1996, p152

[387] Weinstein, 1988 op cit, p76
By contrast Chilean voters approved military rule by a large margin in a 1978 plebiscite.

[388] Weinstein, 1988 op cit, p49

[389] Valenzuela, op cit, pp183, 186-189

[390] Nathaniel Davis, op cit, p374

[391] Grace Livingstone, 'British policy towards the dictatorships of Argentina and Chile 1973 to 1982', University of Cambridge PhD, 2016, pp38-39 - accessed via Google Books 17th February 2020

[392] Ibid, p39

[393] Valenzuela, op cit, p159

[394] Kaufman, op cit, p12

[395] Nathaniel Davis, op cit, pp5, 28 & 94

[396] Ibid, p316

[397] https://www.intelligence.senate.gov/sites/default/files/94chile.pdf - accessed 13th March 2020

[398] Jonathan Haslam, 'The Nixon Administration and the Death of Allende's Chile', 2005

[399] Nathaniel Davis, op cit, pp7 & 8

[400] *Times* 17th September 1974

[401] *Times* 4th February 1974

[402] *Times* 9th September 1974

[403] Nathaniel Davis, op cit,p319

[404] *Times* 26th April 1974

[405] *Times* 5th February 1974

[406] *Times* 11th September 1974

[407] *Times* 16th September 1974

[408] *Times* 28th June 1974

[409] Linz and Stepan, op cit, p206; Diamond et al, op cit, pp196-200
Pinochet received 44% of the vote in a turn-out of 97% of registered voters.

[410] Linz and Stepan, op cit, pp206 & 208

[411] Ibid, p218

[412] Ibid, pp209 & 218

[413] Weinstein, 1988 op cit, p49

[414] *Times* 17th December 1974

[415] Jonathan Hartlyn chapter on Colombia pp291-293 in Diamond et al, op cit

[416] Marco Palacios, 'Between Legitimacy and Violence: A History of Colombia, 1875-2002', 2006, p170

[417] Hartlyn, op cit, p293

[418] Some researchers identify 1974 as the start of civil conflict over land dispossession. See http://www.lse.ac.uk/lacc/publications/PDFs/Sanchez-LopezUribe-OriginOfConflict-03-12-2017.pdf - accessed 31st May 2019

[419] *Times* 19th and 23rd April 1974

López Michelsen appeared in one further article in the newspaper that year, when a story on population growth across the world (including in Colombia) helped fill out the column inches during the UK holiday season (on 19th August 1974).

[420] Hartlyn, op cit, p296

[421] Ibid, pp317 & 326

ANAPO was the subject of a CIA report following the 1970 election and Rojas' near victory. See https://www.cia.gov/library/readingroom/docs/CIA-RDP85T00875R001100090022-3.pdf - accessed 6th March 2020

[422] Palacios, op cit, p171

[423] Jonathan Hartlyn, 'The Politics of Coalition Rule in Colombia', 1988, p138

[424] Palacios, op cit, pp196-197

[425] James Dunkerley, 'Bolivia: Coup d'Etat', Latin America Bureau Special Brief, 1980, p45

[426] Harry E Vanden and Gary Prevost, 'Politics of Latin America: The Power Game', 6th edn., 2018 (orig. 2002), p500

[427] S Sándor John, 'Bolivia's Radical Tradition: Permanent Revolution in the Andes', 2009, pp204-208

[428] Dunkerley, op cit, pp41-43, including: Congress debated US support of $32m between August 1971 and December 1972 and another $60m through USAID in the first year. In addition, US military aid was thrice that of any other Latin American country.

[429] Vanden & Prevost, op cit, p500

[430] Ibid

Also, Sándor John, op cit, p215 and *Times* reports 11th July and 31st August 1974.

[431] Dunkerley, op cit, pp44-47

[432] Ibid, pp49 & 50

[433] https://www.theguardian.com/news/2002/may/06/guardianobituaries.bolivia - accessed 20th March 2020

[434] Vanden & Prevost, op cit, pp501-502

[435] Charles Reilly, 'Peace-Building and Development in Guatemala and Northern Ireland', 2009, p18

[436] Vanden & Prevost, op cit, pp549-553

[437] https://www.independent.co.uk/news/obituaries/general-carlos-arana-osorio-37594.html - accessed 20th March 2020

[438] Vanden and Prevost, op cit, pp578-581

[439] https://api.parliament.uk/historic-hansard/commons/1974/mar/14/aircraft-accident-france#S5CV0870P0_19740314_HOC_73 - accessed 23rd March 2020 Wiggin was addressing the question to the Labour Trade Secretary Peter Shore.

[440] Carol L. Tomeny, "Compensation under the Warsaw Convention for victims of hijackings and terrorist attacks", *Journal of International Law*, 1976. Available at https://brooklynworks.brooklaw.edu/cgi/viewcontent.cgi?article=1451&context=bjil - accessed 23rd March 2020. Notes 18 to 22 are particularly illuminating.

[441] *Times* 10th April 1974, p19

Chapter 10 pp115-122

[442] Robert Bothwell, 'The Penguin History of Canada', 2006, p418

[443] Montreal, Harvard, London School of Economics and the Sorbonne

[444] Bothwell, op cit, p419

[445] Bothwell, op cit, pp403-404

[446] The Liberals had one more seat than the Progressive Conservatives with the New Democratic party holding the balance of power.

[447] Bothwell, op cit, pp427-428

[448] *Times* 10th May 1974

[449] *Times* 15th May 1974

[450] *Times* 9th July 1974

"Party workers say that ... [he] prefers the more philosophical tone he used in 1972."

[451] *Times* 10th July 1974

[452] Divorced in 1984, Margaret Trudeau is now a mental health advocate. She is the mother of the current Canadian Prime Minister Justin Trudeau.

[453] *Times* 25th and 26th October 1974

It should be noted that, on its fortieth anniversary in 2000, EFTA recorded its aim to strike a free trade agreement with Canada. https://www.efta.int/sites/default/files/publications/efta-commemorative-publications/40th-anniversary.pdf - accessed 27th April 2020

[454] Gough Whitlam, 'The Whitlam Government, 1972-1975', 1985, pp182-183

Cited in Stuart Macintyre, 'A Concise History of Australia', 2009 (orig. 1999), p237

[455] *Times* 2nd April 1974

[456] Macintyre, op cit, pp237-239; also Phillip Knightley, 'Australia: A Biography of a Nation', 2001, pp260-261

[457] *Times* 11th April 1974

[458] *Times* 26th and 27th March 1974

In the inimitable and forthright style that might be thought characteristic of Australians, the Minister accompanying Whitlam "blamed 'yahoos and hillbillies who represent the Country Party,'" also referring to the men who threw missiles as "dingoes".

[459] *Times* 15th March 1974

[460] *Times* 18th May 1974

[461] Twenty-nine seats for each of the Labour and Liberal parties, with the balance held by two independents. *Times* 24th June 1974

[462] *Times* 30th May 1974

[463] *Times* 8th August 1974

[464] *Times* 30th and 31st January 1974

[465] The exchange of letters between the Governor-General and Buckingham Palace were released by the National Archives on 14th July 2020. They run to 1282 pages. https://www.theguardian.com/australia-news/ng-interactive/2020/jul/14/the-palace-letters-read-the-full-documents-from-the-national-archives-here - accessed 14th July 2020

Chapter 11 pp123-128

[466] JG Farrell, 'The Singapore Grip', 1978, p57 This is an unusual novel not least in including a bibliography of the historical sources used by Farrell. But then JG Farrell was an unusual writer. Born in Liverpool, he won the 1973 Booker Prize for 'The Siege of Krishnapur' and drowned while fishing in Ireland aged 44 in 1979.

[467] Cadman was one of those appointed by the Postmaster-General Sir Kingsley Wood to the 1932 Bridgeman inquiry into the Post Office. Hugh Gault, 'Kingsley Wood: Scenes from a Political Life 1925-1943', 2017, pp173-177

[468] https://www.theatlantic.com/magazine/archive/1983/03/the-cartel-that-never-was/306495/ -accessed 30th March 2020

[469] Ibid

[470] Kershaw, op cit, p268

[471] Garthoff, op cit, p414 https://history.state.gov/milestones/1969-1976/oil-embargo - accessed 30th March 2020

[472] Both have happened in the Trump presidency 2017-2020, the former deliberately to destabilise Venezuela and the latter inadvertently through the increasing reliance on shale oil in the US.

[473] Maier chapter in Ferguson et al, op cit, p31

[474] https://www.presidency.ucsb.edu/documents/remarks-the-ninth-world-energy-conference-detroit-michigan - accessed 22nd July 2020

[475] Ibid

[476] Robert Skidelsky, 'Money and Government', 2019, pp162-166

[477] Healey, op cit, pp393-394

[478] Macintyre, op cit, pp240-241

[479] National Security Study Memorandums (NSSM), 'Critical Imported Materials: Study of Ad Hoc Group Established by NSSM 197/CIEPSM 33', US Government (Nixon Administration), 1974. Available at the US Bureau

of Public Affairs, Office of the Historian. "Foreign Relations of the United States, 1969–1976, Volume XXXI, Foreign Economic Policy, 1973–1976". https://history.state.gov/historicaldocuments/frus1969-76v31/d260 - accessed 22nd July 2020

Chapter 12 pp129-139

[480] For example, access to water is an increasing dilemma in the twenty-first century as the climate crisis takes hold, but access to clean water remains as insoluble and entrenched a problem for many in the developing world as it was two generations ago.

[481] Quoted in Nathaniel Davis, op cit, p124

[482] Sassoon, op cit, p583

[483] Ibid

[484] Linz and Stepan, op cit, pp117 & 124

[485] Ibid, pp40-65

[486] Sassoon, op cit, is very strong on this political alternation (pp466-467, for example).

[487] That is not to say, of course, that companies do not want to survive into the future but only that their immediate concentration is on growth today. That in fact is the yardstick against which they are judged, regardless of whether it is sustainable.

[488] Allan Patience and Brian Head (eds.), 'From Whitlam to Fraser: Reform and Reaction in Australian Politics', 1979, p287

[489] Butler and Kitzinger, op cit, p2

[490] For example, Lawrence Black and Hugh Pemberton in Lawrence Black, Hugh Pemberton and Pat Thane (eds.), 'Reassessing 1970s Britain', 2013, p9

[491] Pat Thane, 'Divided Kingdom: A History of Britain, 1900 to the Present', 2018, p344

[492] Newitt, op cit, p470

[493] As Greta Thurnberg put it in her September 2019 speech to the UN conference on climate change: "People are suffering. People are dying. Entire ecosystems are collapsing. We are in the beginning of a mass extinction, and all you can talk about is money and fairy tales of eternal economic growth. How dare you!"
Her indictment has a wider resonance in the global turmoil of Covid-19.

[494] Reilly, op cit, p21

[495] Naomi Klein, 'This Changes Everything: Capitalism vs The Climate', 2014 deploys similar arguments.

[496] Morrison, op cit, p.x

[497] Gordon Brown, "In this crisis our leaders must work together. They're failing", *Guardian*, 14th March 2020

BIBLIOGRAPHY

Newspapers
Birmingham Daily Post 24th January and 14th February 1974
Economist 28th July 1973
Guardian 14th March 1975; 14th March 2020
Liverpool Echo 27th December 1974
Times 30th and 31st January, 4th and 5th February, 15th, 26th and 27th
    March, 2nd, 10th, 11th, 19th, 23rd and 26th April, 3rd, 10th, 15th, 18th and
    30th May, 24th and 28th June, 9th, 10th, 11th and 26th July, 8th and 31st
    August, 9th, 11th, 16th, 17th and 25th September, 25th and 26th October,
    17th December 1974; 25th April 1975
Wall Street Journal 24th July 1973

Books

Ayoob, Mohammed (ed.), 'Conflict and Intervention in the Third World',
    London, Croom Helm, 1980

Beller, Steven, 'A Concise History of Austria', Cambridge, Cambridge
    University Press, 2006
Benn, Tony, 'Against the Tide: Diaries 1973-1976', London, Arrow, 1990
    (orig. 1989)
Bew, Paul and Gillespie, Gordon, 'Northern Ireland: A Chronology of the
    Troubles 1968-1993', Dublin, Gill & Macmillan, 1993
Black, Lawrence, Pemberton, Hugh and Thane, Pat (eds.), 'Reassessing
    1970s Britain', Manchester, Manchester University Press, 2013
Bloch, Sidney and Reddaway, Peter, 'Russia's Political Hospitals: The
    Abuse of Psychiatry in the Soviet Union', London, Victor Gollancz,
    1977
Bothwell, Robert, 'The Penguin History of Canada', Ontario, Penguin, 2006
Braunthal, Gerard, 'The West German Social Democrats, 1969-1982:
    Profile of a Party in Power', Boulder, Colorado, Westview Press, 1983
Buckland, Patrick, 'A History of Northern Ireland', Dublin, Gill & Macmillan,
    1981
Butler, David and Kitzinger, Uwe, 'The 1975 Referendum', London,
    Macmillan, 1976

Carr, Jonathan, 'Helmut Schmidt: Helmsman of Germany', London,
    Weidenfeld and Nicolson, 1985
Castle, Barbara, 'The Castle Diaries 1974-1976', London, Weidenfeld &
    Nicolson, 1980
Childs, David (ed.), 'Honecker's Germany', London, Allen & Unwin, 1975
Chomsky, Noam, 'Deterring Democracy', London, Vintage, 1992 (orig.
    1991)

Christie, Iain, 'Machel of Mozambique', Harare, Zimbabwe Publishing House, 1988

Ciment, James, 'Angola and Mozambique: Postcolonial Wars in Southern Africa', New York, Facts on File, 1997

Clogg, Richard, 'A Concise History of Greece', Cambridge, Cambridge University Press, 1992

Davis, Nathaniel, 'The Last Two Years of Salvador Allende', London, IB Tauris, 1985

Davis, William Columbus, 'Warnings from the Far South: Democracy versus Dictatorship in Uruguay, Argentina and Chile', London, Praeger, 1995

Derbyshire, Ian, 'Politics in France: From Giscard to Mitterand', Edinburgh, Chambers, 1990

Diamond, Larry, Linz, Juan and Lipset, Seymour (eds.), 'Democracy in Developing Countries - vol. 4: Latin America', London, Adamantine Press, 1989

Dodd, Clement H, 'The Cyprus Issue: A Current Perspective', Hemingford Grey, Cambs., The Eothen Press, 1994

Dunkerley, James, 'Bolivia: Coup d'Etat', Latin America Bureau Special Brief, London, Latin America Bureau, 1980

El-Mokadem, AM, Hawdon, D, Robinson, C and Stevens, PJ, 'OPEC and the World Oil Market 1973-1983', London, Eastlords Publishing, 1984

Emery, Fred, 'Watergate: The Corruption and Fall of Richard Nixon', London, Jonathan Cape, 1974

Ertekun, NM, 'The Cyprus Dispute and the Birth of the Turkish Republic of Northern Cyprus', Oxford, K Rustem & Brother, 2nd edition, 1984 (orig. 1981)

Farrell, JG, 'The Singapore Grip', London, Weidenfeld and Nicolson, 1978

Ferguson, Niall, Maier, Charles S, Manela, Erez and Sargent, Daniel J (eds.), 'The Shock of the Global: The 1970s in Perspective', London, Belknap, 2010

Fitzmaurice, John, 'Austrian Politics and Society Today: In Defence of Austria', Basingstoke, Macmillan, 1991

Flower, Ken, 'Serving Secretly: Rhodesia's CIO Chief on Record', South Africa, Galago, 1987

Garthoff, Raymond L, 'Détente and Confrontation: American-Soviet Relations from Nixon to Reagan', Washington DC, Brookings Institution, 1985

Gati, Charles, 'The Bloc That Failed: Soviet-East European Relations in Transition', Bloomington, Indiana University Press, 1990

Gault, Hugh 'Kingsley Wood: Scenes from a Political Life 1925-1943', Cambridge, Gretton Books, 2017

Gillespie, Charles, 'Negotiating Democracy: Politicians and Generals in Uruguay', Cambridge, Cambridge University Press, 1991

Godwin, Peter and Hancock, Ian, 'Rhodesians Never Die: The Impact of War and Political Change on White Rhodesia c1970-1980', Oxford, Oxford University Press, 1993

González, Luis, 'Political Structures and Democracy in Uruguay', Notre Dame Indiana, University of Notre Dame Press, 1991

Gregory, Stephen, 'Intellectuals and Left Politics in Uruguay 1958-2006', Eastbourne, Sussex Academic Press, 2009

Haines, Joe, 'Glimmers of Twilight: Harold Wilson in Decline'. London, Politico's, 2003

Hancock, Ian, 'White Liberals, Moderates and Radicals in Rhodesia: 1953-1980', London, Croom Helm, 1984

Harbeson, John W, 'The Ethiopian Transformation: The Quest for the Post-Imperial State', London, Westminster Press, 1988

Hartlyn, Jonathan, 'The Politics of Coalition Rule in Colombia', Cambridge, Cambridge University Press, 1988

Haslam, Jonathan, 'The Nixon Administration and the Death of Allende's Chile', London, Verso, 2005

Healey, Denis, 'The Time of My Life', London, Penguin, 1990 (orig. 1989)

Hitchens, Christopher, 'Cyprus', London, Quartet, 1984

Hodges, Tony, 'Angola from Afro-Stalinism to Petro-Diamond Capitalism', Oxford, James Currey, 2001

Holland, Jack, 'Hope Against History: The Ulster Conflict', London, Hodder & Stoughton, 1999

Janitschek, Hans, 'Mario Soares: Portrait of a Hero', London, Weidenfeld and Nicolson, 1985

Jelavich, Barbara, 'Modern Austria: Empire and Republic, 1815-1986', Cambridge, Cambridge University Press, 1987

John, S Sándor, 'Bolivia's Radical Tradition: Permanent Revolution in the Andes', Tucson, University of Arizona Press, 2009

Katzenstein, Peter J, 'Corporatism and Change: Austria, Switzerland and the Politics of Industry', London, Cornell University Press, 1984

Kaufman, Edy, 'Uruguay in Transition: From Civilian to Military Rule', New Jersey, Transaction Books, 1979

Keller, Edmond J, 'Revolutionary Ethiopia: From Empire to People's Republic', Bloomington, Indiana University Press, 1991

Ker-Lindsay, James, 'The Cyprus Problem', Oxford, Oxford University Press, 2011

Kershaw, Ian, 'Roller-Coaster: Europe 1950-2017', London, Allen Lane, 2018

Klein, Naomi, 'This Changes Everything: Capitalism vs The Climate', London, Allen Lane, 2014

Knightley, Phillip, 'Australia: A Biography of a Nation', London, Vintage, 2001

Kohler, Beate, 'Political Forces in Spain, Greece and Portugal', London, Butterworth Scientific, 1982

Koliopoulos, John S and Veremis, Thanos M, 'Greece: The Modern Sequel from 1821 to the Present', London, Hurst & Co., 2002

Kolko, Gabriel, 'Anatomy of a War: Vietnam, the US and Modern Historical Experience', New York, The New Press, 1994 (orig. 1985)

Latin American Bureau Special Brief, 'Uruguay: Generals Rule', London, Latin American Bureau, 1980

Lefort, René, 'Ethiopia: An Heretical Revolution?', London, Zed Press, 1983 (orig. 1981)

Liebovich, Louis, 'Richard Nixon, Watergate and the Press: A Historical Retrospective', London, Praeger, 2003

Linz, Juan and Stepan, Alfred, 'Problems of Democratic Transition and Consolidation: Southern Europe, South America and Post-Communist Europe', London, John Hopkins University Press, 1996

Macintyre, Stuart, 'A Concise History of Australia', Cambridge, Cambridge University Press, 2009 (orig. 1999)

Mallinson, William, 'Cyprus, A Modern History', London, IB Tauris, 2005

Marshall, Barbara, 'Makers of the Twentieth Century: Willy Brandt', London, Cardinal, 1990

Maxwell, Kenneth, 'The Making of Portuguese Democracy', Cambridge, Cambridge University Press, 1995

Meier, Karl, 'Angola: Promises and Lies', London, Serif/William Waterman Publications, 1996

Meredith, Martin,
    'The Past is Another Country: Rhodesia 1890-1979', London, Andre Deutsch, 1979
    'The State of Africa: A History of Fifty Years of Independence', London, Free Press, 2005

Miard-Delacroix, Helene, 'Willy Brandt: Life of a Statesman', London, IB Tauris, 2016

Möckli, Daniel, 'European Foreign Policy During the Cold War: Heath, Brandt, Pompidou and the Dream of Political Unity', London, IB Tauris, 2009

Morgan, Kenneth O, 'Callaghan: A Life', Oxford, Oxford University Press,1997

Morrison, Rodney J, 'Portugal: Revolutionary Change in an Open Society', Boston Mass., Auburn House Publishing Co., 1981

Newitt, Malyn, 'A History of Mozambique', London, C Hurst & Co., 1995

Palacios, Marco, 'Between Legitimacy and Violence: A History of Colombia, 1875-2002', London, Duke University Press, 2006

Parkes, Stuart, 'Understanding Contemporary Germany', London, Routledge, 1997

Patience, Allan and Head, Brian (eds.), 'From Whitlam to Fraser: Reform and Reaction in Australian Politics', Melbourne, Oxford University Press, 1979

Pimlott, Ben, 'Harold Wilson', London, HarperCollins, 1992

Pine, Melissa, 'Harold Wilson and Europe: Pursuing Britain's Membership of the European Community', London, IB Tauris, 2012

Pittman, Avril, 'From Ostpolitik to Reunification: West German-Soviet Political Relations Since 1974', Cambridge, Cambridge University Press, 1992

Reddaway, John, 'Burdened with Cyprus: The British Connection', London, Weidenfeld & Nicolson, 1986

Reilly, Charles, 'Peace-Building and Development in Guatemala and Northern Ireland', New York, Palgrave Macmillan, 2009

Rubenstein, Joshua, 'Soviet Dissidents: Their Struggle for Human Rights', London, Wildwood House, 1981

Salitan, Laurie P, 'Politics and Nationality in Contemporary Soviet-Jewish Emigration, 1965-1989', Basingstoke, Macmillan, 1992

Sassoon, Donald, 'One Hundred Years of Socialism: The West European Left in the Twentieth Century', London, IB Tauris, 2019 (orig. 1996)

Saunders, Robert, 'Yes to Europe: The 1975 Referendum and Seventies Britain', Cambridge, Cambridge University Press, 2018

Schmidt, Helmut, 'A Grand Strategy for the West: The Anachronism of National Strategies in an Interdependent World', London, Yale University Press, 1985

Shonfield, Andrew, 'Modern Capitalism: The Changing Balance of Public and Private Power', London, Oxford Uuniversity Press, 1965

Short, Philip, 'Mitterand: A Study in Ambiguity', London, Bodley Head, 2013

Silverman, Roger, 'Defiance: Greece and Europe', Winchester, Zero Books, 2016

Skidelsky, Robert, 'Money and Government', London, Penguin, 2019

Smith, Gordon, Paterson, William E and Merkl, Peter H (eds), 'Developments in West German Politics', Basingstoke, Macmillan, 1989

Solzhenitsyn, Alexander, 'Détente: Prospects for Democracy and Dictatorship', New Brunswick, New Jersey, Transaction Books, 1976

Spohr, Kristina, 'The Global Chancellor: Helmut Schmidt and the Reshaping of the International Order', Oxford, Oxford University Press, 2016

Stockwell, John, 'In Search of Enemies: A CIA Story', London, Andre Deutsch, 1978

Thane, Pat, 'Divided Kingdom: A History of Britain, 1900 to the Present', Cambridge, Cambridge University Press, 2018
Tompson, William, 'The Soviet Union Under Brezhnev', London, Pearson, 2003
Tvedten, Inge, 'Angola: Struggle for Peace and Reconstruction', Colorado, Westview Press, 1997

Vanden, Harry E and Prevost, Gary, 'Politics of Latin America: The Power Game', 6th edn., Oxford, Oxford University Press, 2018 (orig. 2002)

Weinstein, Martin,
    'Uruguay: Democracy at the Crossroads', London, Westview Press, 1988
    'Uruguay: The Politics of Failure', London, Greenwood Press, 1975
Whitlam, Gough, 'The Whitlam Government, 1972-1975', Melbourne, Penguin Books, 1985
Wilson, Harold, 'Final Term: The Labour Government 1974-1976', London, Weidenfeld & Nicolson, 1979
Woodhouse, CM, 'Karamanlis: The Restorer of Greek Democracy', Oxford, Clarendon Press, 1982

Articles and Dissertations

Livingstone, Grace, 'British policy towards the dictatorships of Argentina and Chile 1973 to 1982', University of Cambridge PhD, 2016
McBride, Jim, "Civil rights 1968 and Northern Ireland", *The Historian*, Winter 2018-19, 140, pp8-12
Mandelbaum, Michael, "Ending the Cold War", *Foreign Affairs*, Spring 1989
Tomeny, Carol L., "Compensation under the Warsaw Convention for victims of hijackings and terrorist attacks", *Journal of International Law*, 1976

Websites

Australia (and dismissal of Gough Whitlam as Prime Minister)
    www.theguardian.com/australia-news/ng-interactive/2020/jul/14/the-palace-letters-read-the-full-documents-from-the-national-archives-here
Austria www.austria.org/austria-in-the-eu
Bolivia (and Banzer obituary)
    www.theguardian.com/news/2002/may/06/guardianobituaries.bolivia
(Willy) Brandt www.willy-brandt-biography.com/politics/socialist-international/

www.brandt21forum.info/About_BrandtCommission.htm
Chile Population www.populationpyramid.net/chile/1974/
Colombia www.lse.ac.uk/lacc/publications/PDFs/Sanchez-LopezUribe-
    OriginOfConflict-03-12-2017.pdf
    www.cia.gov/library/readingroom/docs/CIA-
    RDP85T00875R001100090022-3.pdf
Conference on Security Co-operation in Europe (Helsinki)
    www.csce.gov/about-csce/helsinki-process-and-osce
Ethiopia //addisstandard.com/news-ethiopian-authorities-deport-prominent-
    scholar-rene-lefort-from-airport-no-explanation/
    www.youtube.com/watch?v=ML32CeRUglU
European Free Trade Area (EFTA)
    www.efta.int/sites/default/files/publications/efta-commemorative-
    publications/40th-anniversary.pdf
European Union (EU, previously EEC) europa.eu/european-union/about-
    eu/countries_en#tab-0-1
    www.consilium.europa.eu/en/council-eu/voting-system/unanimity/
Greece
- Junta 1967-1974 www.ahistoryofgreece.com/junta.htm
- Karamanlis sites.google.com/site/standraenos/the-karamanlis-solution-
    and-the-crisis-of-1965-1967
Guatemala
- Carlos Arana Osorio obituary
    www.independent.co.uk/news/obituaries/general-carlos-arana-osorio-
    37594.html
- Convention api.parliament.uk/historic-
    hansard/commons/1974/mar/14/aircraft-accident-
    france#S5CV0870P0_19740314_HOC_73
Mozambique www.aljazeera.com/news/2019/08/mozambique-president-
    renamo-leader-sign-peace-deal-190801115411693.html
North Atlantic Treaty Organisation (NATO)
    www.nato.int/cps/en/natohq/topics_52044.htm
Northern Ireland Good Friday Agreement www.britannica.com/topic/Good-
    Friday-Agreement
OECD Statistics stats.oecd.org/Index.aspx?DatasetCode=SNA_TABLE1#
Organisation of the Petroleum Exporting Countries (OPEC)
    www.theatlantic.com/magazine/archive/1983/03/the-cartel-that-never-
    was/306495/
    history.state.gov/milestones/1969-1976/oil-embargo
Overseas Development Institute www.odi.org/sites/odi.org.uk/files/odi-
    assets/publications-opinion-files/6827.pdf
Referenda blogs.lse.ac.uk/brexit/2019/08/20/the-risks-of-simple-majority-
    referendums-learning-from-quebec/
Union of Soviet Socialist Republics (USSR or Soviet Union)
- Brezhnev visit to Cuba www.nytimes.com/1974/01/30/archives/brezhnev-
    hailed-by-castro-in-cubaa-soviet-leader-told-cubans-will.html

- Population
  www.census.gov/content/dam/Census/library/publications/1991/demo/ussr.pdf
United Nations www.un.org/en/sections/member-states/growth-united-nations-membership-1945-present/index.html
United States
- Congress hearings on stagflation
  fraser.stlouisfed.org/files/docs/historical/federal%20reserve%20history/Stagflation_051979.pdf
- House of Representatives hearings on human rights in Uruguay and Paraguay
  books.google.co.uk/books?id=PepgxVkkinIC&pg=PP3&lpg=PP3&dq=%22Edy+Kaufman%22+AND+%22Martin+Weinstein%22&source=bl&ots=91o7sjxlmc&sig=ACfU3U3yo2TtggmoaFNaLyIMMKeT8LmWZA&hl=en&sa=X&ved=2ahUKEwj_-e2z_7nnAhVUnVwKHenjDBQQ6AEwAHoECAgQAQ#v=onepage&q=%22Edy%20Kaufman%22%20AND%20%22Martin%20Weinstein%22&f=false
- Pentagon Papers www.nytimes.com/2017/12/20/us/pentagon-papers-post.html
- Population www.censusscope.org/us/chart_popl.html
- Senate Clark Amendment
  academic.brooklyn.cuny.edu/history/johnson/clark.htm
  www.cia.gov/library/readingroom/docs/CIA-RDP85T00287R000400320001-4.pdf
- Senate report on Covert action in Chile
  www.intelligence.senate.gov/sites/default/files/94chile.pdf
Uruguay
- Amnesty International report
  www.amnesty.org/download/Documents/204000/amr520131979en.pdf
- Bordaberry obituary www.theguardian.com/world/2011/jul/19/juan-maria-bordaberry-obituary
- Population www.populationpyramid.net/uruguay/1974/
- Seregni obituary
  www.theguardian.com/news/2004/aug/14/guardianobituaries
Vietnam Population www.cia.gov/library/readingroom/docs/CIA-RDP85T00875R001900010212-2.pdf
(Raoul) Wallenberg www.theguardian.com/world/2019/sep/23/raoul-wallenberg-family-of-diplomat-who-saved-hungarian-jews
Warsaw Convention
  brooklynworks.brooklaw.edu/cgi/viewcontent.cgi?article=1451&context=bjil
West Germany
  www.bundesverfassungsgericht.de/SharedDocs/Entscheidungen/EN/2005/08/es20050825_2bve000405en.html

Photographs on front cover

Constantine Karamanlis

Greece

Gough Whitlam

Australia

Sheikh Yamani

OPEC

Salvador Allende

Chile

Georges Pompidou

France

Costa Gomes

Portugal

Bruno Kreisky

Austria

Archbishop Makarios

Cyprus

Muhammad Ali

USA

Ho Chi Minh

Vietnam

Alexander Solzhenitsyn

USSR

Alfonso López Michelsen

Colombia

Willy Brandt

West Germany

Juan Maria Bordaberry

Uruguay

Richard Nixon

USA

Harold Wilson

UK

Augusto Pinochet

Chile

Samora Machel

Mozambique

Haile Selassie

Ethiopia

Marcello Caetano

Portugal

Pierre Trudeau

Canada

Agostinho Neto

Angola

Leonid Brezhnev

USSR

Hugo Banzer

Bolivia

Front cover photographs

Ian Smith

Rhodesia

Giscard d'Estaing

France

Andrei Sakharov

USSR

Mengistu Haile Mariam

Ethiopia

Gerald Ford

USA

Helmut Schmidt

West Germany

Georgios Papadopoulos and other two members of Junta

Greece